ƒP

Also by CAROLINE MYSS

Anatomy of the Spirit

Why People Don't Heal and How They Can

Sacred Contracts

Creation of Health
(with C. Norman Shealy, M.D., Ph.D.)

Invisible Acts
of Power

PERSONAL CHOICES THAT
CREATE MIRACLES

Caroline Myss

FREE PRESS
NEW YORK · LONDON · TORONTO · SYDNEY

FREE PRESS
A Division of Simon & Schuster, Inc.
1230 Avenue of the Americas
New York, NY 10020

Free Press and colophon are trademarks
of Simon & Schuster, Inc.

For information about special discounts for bulk purchases,
please contact Simon & Schuster Special Sales:
1-800-456-6798 or business@simonandschuster.com

Designed by Julie Schroeder

Manufactured in the United States of America

1   3   5   7   9   10   8   6   4   2

Library of Congress Cataloging-in-Publication Data
Myss, Caroline M.
Invisible acts of power: personal choices that create miracles / Caroline Myss.
p.   cm.
Includes index.
1. Helping behavior—Religious aspects.   2. Spiritual life.
I. Title.
BL629.5.H44 M97 2004
205'.677—dc22   2004053334

ISBN 0-7432-6425-8

To David Smith,
a dear friend and colleague,
with heartfelt gratitude

Contents

Acknowledgments

I am deeply grateful to the many people who contributed their letters to this book. While I was unable to use the more than twelve hundred wonderful stories submitted by all these gracious individuals, rest assured that their spirit and their influence is on every page of this book. I can never thank these individuals as much as they deserve, for they have changed my own life more than I can say, as I hope they will change yours.

And to my forever editor, brilliant Leslie Meredith, my boundless gratitude, love, and appreciation for being my "creative mate" for more than ten years. Without the support of an editor who has a soul filled with vision, dedication to our projects, and faith in their outcome, this book, among all the others we have done together, would not have turned out to be such an inspiration. My heartfelt love and appreciation also goes to Ned Leavitt, my agent, for his constant support of this book along with all my other ideas. He is indeed a patient man. And my great thanks to Dominick Anfuso, Editorial Director, who is such a positive and warm person to have on the Free Press creative support team, and Martha Levin, my champion and Publisher; Suzanne Donahue, Associate Publisher; Carisa Hays, Director of Publicity; and Cassie Dendurent Nelson, Publicity Manager.

My dear sister-in-law, Amy, who has become my sister, deserves more than my love and thanks for her devotion to my work. She supplies all the organizational skills I will never have and a dedication to perfection and details that allowed me to relax into the creative process. She is a right hand, a colleague, and a trusted friend.

Tami Simon, owner of Sounds True Productions in Boulder, Colorado, deserves more than my thanks for converting the text of this book to an audio series.

I have a dear and precious circle of friends, all of whom helped so much with their insights and support, whom I thank so very much with deep love and affection: Michael Gluck, Mary Neville, Penny Tompkins, Donald McKay, Penny Simon, Chandra Sammons, Lynn Bell, Jim Curtan, Pat Pilkington, Dawn Jiosi, Charles and Sue Wells, Barbara Porter, Kathy Musker, Ingrid Williams, Meryl Martin, Prentiss Prevette, Maureen Connolly-King, Sue Marco, and Peter Occhiogrosso. I also thank Andy Bettis for the use of his office and computer while in Findhorn, Scotland, during the final, desperate days of working to meet the deadline. My gratitude also goes to Ted Falkiewicz, Peter Harlan and Gail Prauss, who organized their activities and schedules around mine in order to support the demands of my writing schedule.

And with great love and devotion I thank my Earth Angels, without whom life would be a very difficult journey: my mom and my brother, Ed. Some people you love more than can be measured in words. I could never adequately describe how much my mother and my brother mean to me. I am blessed with a wonderful and loving family that also includes these Earth Angels: my dear friend, Donald Meshirer, my cousins, Pam and Andy Kruzel, Marilyn and Mitch Kaminski, Colleen Daley, and Chris and Richard Witek, who never cease to be a positive force in my heart and spirit. My nieces and nephews, who showed up late at night with "instant message" support, checking in to see how "Auntie" was doing, are more loved and appreciated by me than they will ever know: Angela, Allison, Joe, Rachel, Sarah, and Eddie. And finally, my creative Earth Angels who share the day-to-day rigors of my life and help me to succeed and survive the demands of my life: my business colleague and dear friend, David Smith, and my devoted assistant, Judy Haskett, who has been with me for years. Without Judy, my professional life would be even more ungrounded and chaotic than it is. Again, with the deepest thanks and so much love, I thank each of you once more.

Introduction

When I was growing up Roman Catholic, we were bilingual in English and angels. Miracles could happen every day. The invisible power of angels and saints was everywhere and their existence was a given, a fact, ordinary. It would have been unthinkable *not* to believe in them.

Every day was a saint's day and gave us the opportunity to recognize the importance of a particular virtue or energy that each saint embodied. We regularly invoked the saints' and angels' strengths: St. Jude gave us the courage to face impossible causes; St. Anthony helped us notice and find lost objects; St. Francis protected our animals and taught us compassion for all life. Even as an adult, when I was selling my home recently and wanted to make it go as fast as possible, I borrowed a statue of St. Joseph from a close childhood friend and, according to tradition, buried it upside down in the backyard. Say what you will, but my house sold within days of that little ritual.

For some of us children, the angels and saints were our first brush with invisible power. These nonphysical beings peopled our spiritual world and surrounded us with their support. We were never alone, and when we called or prayed to them, they always answered. They were our first spiritual community. Their lives modeled the power of faith—proof that no physical force on earth, from political oppression to illness, could defeat heaven.

To this day, the saints and angels are invisible forces in my life. Yet I also have a faith in an even greater power: the energy, or grace, that animates our seemingly impersonal but intimately interconnected universe. We receive infusions of grace on a daily basis, but in the middle of the everyday tasks of making a living and taking care of our family and friends, we can miss its subtle power. Grace holds together the whole of our life—and all of our lives collectively. It watches over us and will come to our aid if we ask.

Many times I have wished that I could convince others to have faith in this immeasurable, invisible force that surrounds and protects us. I feel profound bliss in knowing that even in the direst times, our prayers are heard and answered. I have seen and experienced far too many miracles to believe otherwise. Like you, I've had to move mountains in my personal and professional life. Whenever I am striving mightily on my own, pushing and getting nowhere, I usually realize that it's time to step back and remember that, "If ye have faith as a grain of mustard seed, ye shall say unto this mountain, / Remove hence to yonder place; and it shall remove." As the Tao Te Ching also advises, "Do your work, then step back. The only path to serenity." Nothing is impossible for you when you have faith—in yourself and in your purpose.

Faith is an active force—not a passive one—an invisible power, like love. It is not simply a belief in goodness, it is a belief put into action in the present moment. In the ancient Hindu belief system, faith also conveys protection, by giving us trust and confidence in the rightness of what we are doing. Faith enables us to have a positive attitude and hope even in the face of seemingly irreversible setbacks.

God works anonymously—invisibly—through these powers of faith, love, and grace. Perhaps this is because we humans are too meddlesome to be trusted with a direct divine intervention. Remember that mortals in ancient mythology who looked directly at a god (who was not disguised in an earthly form) went blind or mad from the sight. God frequently sends divine grace through human agents who perform nonrandom acts of kindness.

As I often tell the people who study spirituality and intuition with me in my workshops, we are all born here to go to Earth School. We're on this planet to learn to be spiritual beings in a physical body, to gain consciousness of our greater purpose. Life on Earth is all about learning to manage your power. So this book is a course in Earth School about managing your personal power in a way that enhances your own spiritual growth, while also contributing to the evolution of the people around you—and to the entire global soul.

Giving and receiving are learned arts. As children, we first learn to give and to receive in visible ways—we're fed, clothed, and sheltered and we learn to feed, clothe, nourish, and care for others. As we mature, we undertake other vital acts of caring—we serve as listeners to our friends and loved ones; we encourage them and pray for them; we grow in our effectiveness in the world and learn to help and empower others.

Learning to manage your personal power means that you have to become aware of how you work with your energy and whom you give it to. "Those who overcome themselves are strong," wrote Lao-tzu. It's also about how much you are willing to surrender to divine guidance, which often comes to you in the guise of inner intuition. By finding your inner compass and acting on its promptings, you come into your full power and fulfill the life mission you were born to complete. I call this mission your Sacred Contract and it includes not just the daily work you do, but every relationship you have and every person you meet, everyone you help, and everyone who helps you.

*   *   *

Oftentimes, an author does not know how to begin a book, but I found it difficult to end this one. When I began, I had intended to write a simple examination of how we are called into action to help each other. Yet the writing grew into a personal spiritual awakening for me. In my previous books, my intention was always to teach a new method of seeing and understanding your spirit and your life. In this book, I want to do that *and* I also want to make you redefine your view of power in this world. I want to help you realize that no matter how much money you have, no matter what sex, race, or age you are, you *do* have power. You *can* make a difference in your world and in the life of every single person you encounter.

In the course of writing this book, I solicited stories from readers and subscribers to my Web site about their experiences with grace and life-changing acts of service. I was honored and overwhelmed to receive twelve hundred letters within six days of making my request. I discovered that it is one thing to talk abstractly about human goodness and our potential to be kind, but it's quite another to come into direct contact with hundreds of real stories of real people exercising their power to heal, to help each other, to make a difference. I felt saturated in the caring and warmth of being human that these stories convey. They are solid evidence that the great power of compassion, honor, and grace still exists, even in the middle of national and world crises. They also prove that we are not alone in this world and that even in the direst times, our prayers are heard and answered.

I have worked as an intuitive for more than two decades and have been teaching others how to develop their own intuition for more than ten years. The main thing that I stress with my students is that they—you—are already intuitive. But you have to open yourself to the messages that you are receiving. Many people resist hearing the messages their intuition sends them, often because they don't want to deal with the changes that they would have to make if they listened and acted on the guidance. But these stories demonstrate that we really *can* make a profound difference when we listen to our intuition and act on it. And I give you instructions on how to notice and follow your intuition in each chapter.

These stories show that everything we do *counts*. There is really no such thing as a small act of service or goodness. This is in accord with most of the world's spiritual traditions. The Tao Te Ching advises, "Do the great while it is still small." And the philosopher and social activist Martin Buber writes, "The things that happen to me day after day, the things that claim me day after day—these contain my essential task." Every day we are called to perform large and small acts of courage and grace. And the effects of every small action are multiplied a thousandfold. The Buddha taught, "Happiness is the accumulation of good."

Every time someone says, "God, please help me," the universe hears. The gods may let you practically drown before they respond and send you a boat—because you are in this Earth School to learn how to build a boat *and* how to row it—but they *will* respond. The power of a single wish can change your life. And once you ask, once you open your mind and heart to the possibility of an answer, you will get an answer, even though it may not be the one you want or in the form you expect.

These stories prove how intimate our seemingly impersonal universe is and how interconnected we are. Through them, I have discovered an invisible spiritual community of physical angels. These angels masquerade as our friends, family, and often and especially strangers. They are all around us and they appear at the right time, often in the nick of time, to help us when we are in need. They create meaning and hope where before there was pain and despair. Like the people in these stories, you, too, have an invisible spiritual community that supports you, but you also have the power to go out and create more meaning and goodness—more nonrandom acts of kindness. And of course the good that you create inevitably comes back to you.

Before I had even thought about asking my readers to send me their stories, I had wanted to put together a list of acts of service for my Web site. This was to be my own personal act of service. Partly it was in response to my students telling me that people need to feel good about other people again; these stories certainly do that for me. And partly it was in response to the thousands of people I have met through the years who are searching for a path that gives their life meaning and purpose. Among the many aspects of life that give us meaning, helping others is one of the most rewarding. Indeed, the need to be of service has evolved into a spiritual necessity for many people, perhaps as a result of our living longer and desiring to remain active in society and purposeful through our entire life. I rarely meet people who want to retire from a meaningful life.

People in their middle years, especially, seek out meaning. Carl Jung described maturity as an awakening to the need to live a life of spiritual purpose rather than simply fulfilling the basic needs of physical survival or pursuing pleasure. He saw each person as the hero of his or her own life's journey who sets out on a path to greater spiritual awareness. The one thousand two hundred plus letters that I received show that not only do many people have a hunger for spiritual connection, they also have created a personal theology of service and healing, a feeling of responsibility for their fellow man. They are an invisible community of heroes.

Even knowing this, however, I had not considered, before writing this book, that caring for others and going that extra mile for family, friends, coworkers, or strangers could have a connection to our physical health. Now I believe that the human spirit needs to develop generosity and compassion to be healthy. We need to respond to others' vulnerabilities in the process of addressing and healing our own. Exercising empathy and compassion and performing good deeds makes our body and spirit thrive. One scientific study, for instance, found that an effective way to find relief from our own stress and strains is to pray for others. Another study revealed that we require at least four hours a month of face-to-face volunteering for good health. Numerous other studies have shown that positive emotions cause greater activity in the brain and increase the antibodies that fight disease. In other words, helping others promotes our own wellness. Our bodies actually thank us for reaching out!

Health is not just the slowest possible rate at which one can die, as some cynics say. The warm glow we get from helping others is not just a good physical feeling—it is the energy of a healing grace that moves between the giver and the receiver and blesses both. We need each other. We're not meant to be completely independent, but to give and receive. You cannot increase in self-understanding and well-being and simultaneously remain isolated from humanity. You cannot strive for a healthier, more spiritual life if you keep yourself separate and apart from life around you. The journey of the "self" also involves the journey of the "other."

We've always known this to be true; world literature is rich with stories that reflect this essential human principle. In *The Odyssey*, Ulysses returns home disguised as a beggar to see whether his subjects are decent human beings and how they treat a stranger in their midst. Shiva, the god of many forms, wanders the world in rags, representing that God is everywhere and can be found in any and every situation, testing us mortals in our ability to recognize our connection with every being on earth. Dickens's *A Christmas Carol* shows the necessity of awakening to the power of generosity and goodness and its lifesaving consequences for the giver and the receiver.

The many people whose life experiences fill the pages of this book remind us to heed the call to be of service to one another. Like characters in their own life stories, they survived, endured, and thrived because a modest hero reached out with a gift of grace when they needed it most. They faced and overcame serious problems, discovering in the process how deeply valued they are. These stories remind us again and again that we are not alone. They renew our faith in a guiding force greater than ourselves. And as we read them, we understand that this grace that happens to others—interventions, spontaneous healings, or the kindness of strangers—can also happen to us.

These stories are an absolute pleasure to share with you. I loved every second of writing this book and often ended up in tears in response to the love, compassion, sweetness, and faith of the people who wrote to me. I am so grateful to them, more than I can express. While I regret not being able to use all the letters submitted to me for this book, I did use all of them as I organized the material, which helped me arrive at the insights I present. For me, this book was a personal spiritual journey in which a theory of goodness incarnated into the grace of experience.

I hope that these stories warm and inspire you as much as they did me. I hope that they sustain you with hope and faith when difficult times occur in your own life. And I also hope that the life experiences of these individuals will help you to realize how much power you have as an individual to make a difference in the life of every person you meet—through your own invisible acts of power.

The Stages
of Power

Grace, Intuition, and Power

*Your neighbor is your other self dwelling behind a wall. In under-
standing, all walls shall fall down. Who knows but that your neighbor
is your better self wearing another body? See that you love him as you
would yourself. He too is a manifestation of the Most High.*

— KAHLIL GIBRAN

One evening during the summer, as I was sitting on my balcony, I noticed a young man waiting at the bus stop across the street from my home. He was about seventeen years old and dressed in every way that makes me nuts. His slacks were dragging on the concrete, completely covering his feet. I counted three tattoos on his muscled arms and a complement of pierced ears and eyebrow. Imitating my parents from thirty years ago, I thought, "What is wrong with these kids today? Why do they want to look like that?"

As I was manufacturing my own opinions about this boy, an older woman began to struggle across the street with oversize, heavy boxes. The young man noticed her, too, and, as if it were the most natural instinct in the world, walked over and offered to help her. She gratefully released the boxes into his arms and led him to her car. He placed her belongings in the trunk, nodded, and turned to go, but in the most remarkable, touching way, the woman wrapped her arms around him and gave him a warm bear hug of a thank-you. Then she drove away. He stood smiling a moment and returned to the bus stop. Within a minute of that tender exchange, he was aboard his bus, leaving me alone on my porch to think about the extraordinary encounter I had just witnessed. Perhaps this young man would never think about that older woman again and the favor he had done for her. But the woman certainly would. She had been graced with help that had come out of nowhere just when she needed it.

This encounter struck home with me because two days before, someone had helped me in much the same way. Unlike many lucky travelers, I cannot take carry-on luggage on planes because I cannot lift a great deal of weight. Having learned that I can't take for granted that someone will help me stow baggage overhead, I usually check it—even though it often gets lost between connecting flights. On this particular day, however, my flight connections were so tight that I had to take my luggage on board. For most people, this is no big deal, but for me, the anticipation of lifting suitcases causes me more anxiety than I can communicate. It actually gives me ice-cold hands and a racing pulse; afterward, I usually get excruciating neck, back, and shoulder pain that lasts for days.

As I braced myself in the aisle for the dreaded struggle, the man waiting behind me for his seat simply picked up and tossed my luggage into the overhead compartment. He had helped without my asking, without even knowing how much I needed help. My eyes filled with tears, I was so grateful. I can still see his face flushed with embarrassment as I overreacted with my thanks.

I spent much of that flight thinking how blessed I was by the man's kindness. I was also able to relax for the rest of the flight knowing that he would repeat the favor by taking down my luggage when the plane landed. Because of his help, I would be able to lecture that evening without a sore, inflamed shoulder or back pain to distract me. Even though he would never know any of the reasons for my gratitude, I will always remember him.

In that encounter between the older woman with the boxes and the tattooed young man, I saw myself and my fellow passenger. I realized that what my anonymous friend had done for me was far more than the simple favor of placing my luggage in the overhead: He allowed me to keep my dignity and peace of mind and body. He had performed an invisible act of power and empowerment.

I began to think about how little it takes to do a lot for someone else and about the amazing, long-range consequences of a single thoughtful act. As the ancient Hindu sages realized, the laws of cause and effect are universal and the good and harm we do is eternal. They called this interplay karma: the sum effect of all our actions as well as our decisions not to take action.

What really takes place inside you when you respond to someone in need? Why do some people jump out of their seats to help another person, while others look the other way? No doubt, some people have been taught to be kind and others may be naturally thoughtful. But I think something greater than compassion or good manners is at work, something beyond the motivation of the strong to help the weak or the wealthy to help the poor. I think it is the invisible power of grace, moving between the open hearts of the giver and the receiver. The action itself, the lifting of a heavy piece of luggage or the drink of water offered to the thirsty man, may be small. But the energy that is channeled through that action is the high-voltage current of grace. It contains the power to renew someone's faith in himself. It even has the power to save a life.

These two experiences affected me profoundly. As a result, I decided to do a little project: I would put together a list of suggestions for my e-newsletter about how we all can be of service to others in our day-to-day lives. I also sent out a letter to subscribers on my Web site asking them to share their experiences of being either the receiver or the provider of some form of grace or assistance. I expected to see a hundred letters or so, but within six days I had received one thousand two hundred letters from people from all over the planet. Equally impressive was how many of them said how blessed they still felt by the experience.

I've worked with people for twenty years and have heard thousands of amazing stories of overcoming personal pain and tragedy, so life never ceases to surprise me. But I was completely taken aback by the emotional content of these letters and the manner in which each person so beautifully told his or her story. People wrote about the powerful effect of hearing the right words at the right time, the comfort of a couch for the night, a hug that helped them keep going, the blessing of someone simply sitting with them, listening to them talk or cry. Many people wrote about their gratitude to someone who pitched in for them at work when they needed to be out caring for a family member. Others recalled the favors of friends who had taken over mundane chores and freed them to enjoy a reunion or other celebration. One woman wrote, "Few things meant as much to me as when two of my friends cleaned my house a few days before my wedding."

Some said they felt "divinely protected" all over again as they recalled incidents when they were most desperate and food or money just "appeared." One wrote, "After having a stranger show up at my door with rent money for me and my child one hour before my landlord confronted me with a demand to leave, I never needed proof again that I was being looked after by heaven. This person overheard my weeping at a table in a restaurant when I told my friend that I was desperate because I could no longer protect my daughter. This man, my Good Samaritan, slipped a note to my friend asking her for my name and address.

He showed up at my door that afternoon with $550. Because of him, my daughter was spared the trauma of homelessness and I was spared the loss of my dignity as a mother."

As I organized the huge volume of letters, I looked for three elements in each story: the crisis, the gift, and the consequence. I was particularly interested in the "size" (for lack of a better word) of the help or gift in relation to the "size" of the effect it created. It takes very little to make a profound difference in someone's life, very little. What appeared to be a "hot cup of tea brought to me while I was up late studying," wrote one man, "became the evening ritual of loving support from my wife. That cup of tea was her way of saying that she knew how difficult night school was and that it was okay with her that I no longer had time available for us. That changed, of course, once I graduated, but school could have been an experience of neglect and guilt instead of earning a law degree had it not been for her kindness."

Whether making a cup of tea, cleaning an apartment, or sitting up all night with someone waiting for a medical diagnosis, every one of these experiences is an invisible act of power, a cleverly disguised means through which the vital energy of grace is channeled into someone's life.

Grace

To see a World in a grain of sand,
And a Heaven in a wild flower,
Hold Infinity in the palm of your hand,
And Eternity in an hour.

—WILLIAM BLAKE, "AUGURIES OF INNOCENCE"

Although it is difficult to capture its full nature in one definition, grace is unmistakable when experienced. Grace is a noun and a verb; it is a state and an action, an energy that flows between two beings. Grace is gratis, a gift. In theology, grace is defined as unmerited divine assistance, aid given to help us regenerate our spirits and lives—a virtue coming from God. The concept of grace exists around the world. In secular history, kings, as the representatives of divine power on earth, would grant mercy and pardon, or grace, to their subjects. In Greek mythology, the three graces were sister goddesses, daughters of Zeus, who bestowed joy, charm, and beauty on mortals. We humans are blessed to be both generators and receivers of grace.

I've been fascinated by grace since watching the movies *The Nun's Story* with Audrey Hepburn and *The Sound of Music* with Julie Andrews when they were first released back in the 1960s. Both are stories of young novices who feel great inner conflict about their true calling and question whether they are meant to fulfill that calling in a convent. In both cases, the reverend mother, who directs the communities of nuns, instructs the young women to "pray for grace" that will show them what to do next with their lives. Even as a twelve-year-old girl, I was drawn to this directive to pray for grace. I wondered, "How would she know when grace arrived? What would grace feel like?" Interestingly, both women ended up leaving the convent as a result of their prayers, yet the message that stayed with me was that grace and guidance do come to those who ask for it. And it is not limited by religion, but comes to nuns and other women and girls, men and boys, parents and professionals, and people who have lost their way, as spiritual traditions around the world as well as the letters in this book attest.

When teaching about health and human consciousness, until now I have often defined grace as a universal life force, but now I find that to be inadequate. Life force simply "is." It is a neutral, undirected energy that surrounds us and supports the vitality of all beings. Grace, on the other hand, has a spiritual quality. It is energy infused with a force greater than our own, a divine intention. When it arrives—usually unannounced or unrequested, "out of the blue"—it fills you with a luminous awareness that is different from everyday consciousness; it makes you come alive with vision and determination and the strength to act. Grace is also the organizing force behind "coincidences," the synchronistic experiences in our lives that some consider chance but that are definitely not random.

Grace illuminates your path by moving through your intuition, influencing the choices that you make. When left to our own devices, we often choose to do things that reflect our shadow side—the dark fears and uncertainty about our ability to survive in the physical world. Nonetheless, we always have an awareness, a feeling, or a gut instinct about what we should think, say, or do. When we say, "I don't know what to do," we are rarely being truthful. We most likely don't *want* to do what we are sensing we need to do, but we are, quite frankly, too intuitive to get away with that excuse. We—you—cannot *not* be intuitive. The energy of grace is a relentless internal voice that we can rarely misinterpret or silence. It is a power that works hand in hand with intuition to guide our actions in the right direction— the direction that will do the most good.

Intuition and Power

There are only two ways to live your life. One is as though nothing is a miracle. The other is as if everything is.

—ALBERT EINSTEIN

To understand fully the rich variety of experiences in the one thousand two hundred letters, we have to look at how intuition and personal power work with grace. Intuition is, first of all, an expression of power. It is not a mystical talent to see the future so that you can keep yourself safe. Most people want intuition to protect their backs and act as a sort of life-control and relationship-control device. They want mystical tricks of protection and survival, not necessarily the kind of high-voltage guidance that intuition conveys—the kind that inevitably changes their life. They're looking for spiritual guidance that ensures material accomplishments—a spirituality that has a decidedly material outcome. To many, that spiritual guidance had better be practical and professional, and it better have a pension plan.

The truth is, we all have intuition, but how well we respond to what it tells us to do depends largely on how psychologically and emotionally capable we feel. That feeling—which is also often called self-esteem, self-respect, or self-efficacy—has a direct bearing upon how we relate to other people. Without self-esteem, we build private agendas into everything that we do. An insecure person finds it difficult if not impossible to help someone else because he or she views all others as competitors.

Your intuition automatically reads the energy of everyone around you. Every living being is made up of energy and all of this energy contains information. Your physical body is surrounded by an energy field that is both an information clearing center and a highly sensitive perceptual system. We are constantly communicating with everything around us, with the greater energy of the universe and the consciousness of other living creatures. Our energy field sends and receives messages to and from other people and these internal and external messages form energy impressions that are picked up by our intuition.

These impressions are a kind of energetic language that our intuition recognizes and interprets by running it through the seven "translators" or energy centers in the body. Called *chakras* (pronounced CHUK-ra, an ancient Sanskrit term meaning "wheel"), each center revolves and emits its own frequency. The chakras form our energy anatomy, which works in harmony with our physical anatomy to keep us healthy and functioning. The chakras also connect us to the greater energy field of life and the universe. Our intuition tunes in to the different frequencies of each energy center and frequently alerts us with a feeling or gut instinct that something is wrong, or that our mind, body, and spirit are out of balance.

The chakras also correspond to seven classic stages of spiritual development through which we are meant to go to gain self-understanding. Every culture has its own traditions for how its members are to grow and mature and, basically, to learn how to manage their personal power. Together, these traditions and rites of passage symbolize the universal spiritual journey—the hero's journey, as the great mythologist Joseph Campbell called it.

Each of us, as the hero of our own life, faces different earthly and spiritual challenges from which we learn lessons that allow us to evolve different, increasingly higher qualities of power. All problems, all stresses present an opportunity for spiritual learning in which you can gain insight into the use, misuse, or misdirection of your personal power. For instance, our first life lessons are about how to live within a family; how to accommodate each other and abide by our tribe's rules. Eventually, we undergo initiations into adulthood and learn how to strike out on our own and live within a larger community; we decide whether to rebel against our tribe or remain a part of it; we take a partner; we develop skills, create a livelihood, or enter a profession; we become parents, mentors, masters in our vocations and avocations. As we age, we are also meant to grow in responsibility, in compassion toward others, and in wisdom, understanding, and consciousness.

The chakras, our power centers, symbolize all these steps. Aligned vertically from the base of the spine to the crown of the head, they suggest that we increase in spiritual power as we master the seductive pull of the material world. First identified in the East, the chakra system is the basis for certain Hindu, Buddhist, and Taoist teachings, but it also corresponds to the mystical energy defined by Western traditions. As you will see, the chakras also correspond with the different kinds of grace manifested in the letters in this book.

The chakras form what I call the anatomy of our spirit. The first chakra, at the base of the spine, contains energy that relates to the material world, to concerns of basic survival. The second chakra, located just below the waist, teaches lessons related to the energy of sexuality, work, and creativity, as well as self-protection. The third chakra, at the solar plexus, concerns issues related to the ego, individual personality, and self-esteem. The fourth chakra, the heart chakra, governs our exercise of love, compassion, and forgiveness. The fifth is related to the power of our will and self-expression. The sixth governs our mind, rational thought, insight, and wisdom. The seventh is our spiritual connection to the universe. So you see, the direction of our spiritual development is "up": we move from first learning how to survive in the world—to eat, shelter, and protect our individual selves—to seeing our unity with all life, to connecting with each other and with the divine.

While our spirit matures and moves upward, the energy of grace comes down from above. The two forces spiral around each other and through the chakras like an energetic double helix. Grace actually flows into us through our seventh chakra, the spiritual circuit. Then it merges with the rational thought of our sixth chakra, motivates our will in our fifth chakra, and penetrates into the heart center for an emotional response. Our third chakra personalizes the energy; those personal feelings pour into our second chakra, which shapes our response into an action as it also tries to make sure we are safe in our response.

Finally, the energy that began as inspiration and grace in the seventh chakra becomes grounded in our first chakra, connecting us to the earth, the moment. The chakras form our spiritual lightning rod, grounding the electric energy of grace into our beings and our bodies.

As I considered how grace, intuition, and power worked together in the stories of the people who wrote me, I noticed that most of the writers quite unconsciously categorized their letters for me by using the same or similar turns of phrases. For example, people who received assistance out of nowhere from a stranger referred to either the person or his or her story as "The Good Samaritan." After I organized all the letters, seven categories emerged.

7 Once Again

Sometimes you just can't get away from certain things. I am constantly tripping over the number 7: there are 7 chakras, 7 holy sacraments in Christianity, 7 major energy categories in Western mysticism. Someone orders 7 UP in a restaurant and I almost do an intuitive reading. So naturally when seven categories emerged out of one thousand two hundred letters, I wanted to see if they might correspond with the meaning of the chakras. At first I did this out of curiosity, not really expecting that I'd find a new perspective on the architecture of the human energy system. Yet when I finished this little exercise, I discovered that just as there is a hierarchy of power, there is also a hierarchy of grace. And I realized that the call to be of service to one another, the intuition that prompts us to use our power to help others, is wired into our physical and spiritual nature.

Here is how acts of service correspond to energies of the chakras, with physical help corresponding to the first chakra:

CHAKRA ONE: the Root Chakra: Gifts of the Earth—
                Food and Shelter
CHAKRA TWO: the Energy of Self-Protection: Gifts of
                Survival—Financial and Creative Support
CHAKRA THREE: Ego Energy: Gifts of Self-Esteem—
                Unconditional Support, Friendship, and
                Personal Dignity
CHAKRA FOUR: the Heart Chakra: Gifts of the Heart—
                Kindness, Love, Forgiveness, and
                Compassion
CHAKRA FIVE: the Energy of Determination: Gifts of
                Will—Courage and Guidance
CHAKRA SIX: the Energy of Rational Thought: Gifts
                of the Mind—Wisdom and Optimism
CHAKRA SEVEN: the Center of Higher Consciousness:
                Gifts of the Spirit—Angels in Disguise
                and Good Samaritans

CHAKRA ONE, THE ROOT CHAKRA:
Gifts of the Earth—Food and Shelter

Your first chakra is the anchor that connects you and your spirit to your physical life and the physical world. Its energy is located at the base of the spine and includes your home, family, support system, and social connections. Think of this chakra as your backbone, your "earth ID," your magnetic locator or Global Positioning System. It provides you with your physical coordinates—a group or tribal identity, a culture, heritage, and religious and other traditions. This chakra grounds you and identifies you with a place and a people; it connects you to somewhere and someone; it answers the question, "Who am I?" This energy likes consistency, a sense of security and well-being. It builds tribal self-esteem rather than individual, independent identity.

Food, shelter, clothing, a job, and core relationships such as family and close friends form the base of a stable life. Without these anchors, it is almost impossible to do anything else with your life. A person who must struggle to find a meal every day, for instance, has great difficulty envisioning a future that is free from want. To people who are homeless or have been homeless, gifts of shelter and food—first-chakra acts of power—are actually a second chance at life. Being disconnected from the place on earth you call home is traumatic, and the homeless and hungry are often emotionally shattered and physically and financially desperate; reconnecting to that fundamental life current requires help.

CHAKRA TWO, THE ENERGY OF
SELF-PROTECTION:

Gifts of Survival—Financial and Creative Support

Your second chakra oversees "what's mine"—your personal belongings, relationships, and partnerships. This second phase of earthly power represents growing up out of the roots of your tribal or group identity and into your ability to provide for yourself. Second-chakra energy is rugged, determined, resilient, survival oriented, sexual, and creative. Its energetic ingredients help us meet and master all kinds of life challenges, from first surviving within a family or apart from our tribe of origin, to forging a sexual identity and creating children, to developing street smarts and business savvy, to recovering from setbacks. The second chakra also involves the energy of money, of making money and working with money.

The second chakra is the seat of your creative as well as your procreative energy. Creativity is often misapprehended as a purely artistic or intellectual inclination (that's a more mental energy associated with the sixth chakra), but working with your creative energy is as essential to your health and overall well-being as breathing and eating. Creative energy is a basic survival instinct; it motivates us to become part of society, to become productive, to bring things to life, and to distinguish ourselves from others by what we make, the crafts we pursue, the skills we develop in business or in cultivating friendships, the entrepreneurial ideas we conceive, the problems we resolve, and the children or communities we birth and nurture. Yet many people have creative ideas and yearnings that they do not pursue out of a fear of financial failure or embarrassment, or because they are reluctant to step outside of their normal way of life and change it. They abort their dreams, not realizing that psychological and emotional abortions can be more devastating than physical ones. As a medical intuitive, I have seen many depressions and other chronic suffering at whose source was the repression and denial of a strong creative urge.

Some people struggle to find the help they need to get an idea off the ground. Others have suffered personal tragedies that have ruined their finances and can barely keep their or their families' body and soul together. In the letters I received, the writers recalled their gratitude for gifts of financial support, a classic second-chakra gift, but most often they noted that these acts of generosity also helped them to come alive again creatively—an invisible consequence that their benefactors may not have foreseen.

CHAKRA THREE, EGO ENERGY:
Gifts of Self-Esteem—Unconditional Support, Friendship, and Personal Dignity

The third chakra is the center of self-esteem and personal power, of honor and ethics. Its energy infuses you with the sense of "what I am" as opposed to "who I am" as in the first chakra— it's a center of doing as well as of being. This is the "hara" or "vital center" according to some Eastern philosophies: the seat of personal strength, healthy psychological boundaries, and self-sufficiency, the solar plexus. This is also where we generate the ability to make decisions for ourselves, to handle crises and take risks.

In many ways, this chakra is the most influential over our ability to create a happy, satisfying life. An individual who believes in himself feels that the world is a beneficent place—or at least not a threatening, frightening place. He or she is not scared by the challenges life brings and has an inner security that money cannot buy. Someone with no self-esteem cannot fill that void with all the money in the world. He or she will never be happy, secure, or free from fear. It is possible, of course, to survive in this world without self-esteem, but it is impossible to have an inner sense of freedom and security—to be happy—without this fundamental sense.

We want to feel good about who we are even more than we want to feel good about what we have. But until we gain self-esteem, we will always feel socially and spiritually vulnerable, and focus on belongings and power plays rather than on our inner power. We will measure our success by how much we control the external world and other people. We will be vulnerable to others' control of our attitudes, thoughts, dreams, or ambitions. We will even fear the power of God—especially God's invisible power to change every aspect of our life—and doubt our own abilities to improve our lives and others'. Every time we choose to enhance our internal power, however, we limit the authority of the physical world over our lives, bodies, health, minds, and spirits.

Acts of service that nurture an individual's self-esteem are literally lifesavers. Praise, respect, and appreciation; the patient giving of advice or teaching of a skill to help someone get ahead; bucking up someone's spirits after she has lost hope—these are all third-chakra gifts of power. And they last forever. As some of the letter writers noted, "It just took a second and I felt better," and, "One smile from a stranger saved my life." This kind of third-chakra act of service—empowerment—is measured by your sincerity, not by how much energy or money or time you expend.

With each ascending chakra, the acts of service become more energy based, or "energetic," as I call them, more spiritual and less physical—but more powerful.

CHAKRA FOUR, THE HEART CHAKRA:

Gifts of the Heart—Kindness, Love, Forgiveness, and Compassion

Your fourth chakra is aligned to your emotional life and is the center of your emotional well-being. This energy answers the question, "Whom shall I love and how shall I love?" Acts of kindness, love, forgiveness, and compassion can do more in five minutes to heal or nurture someone than ten thousand dollars' worth of therapy spread over a year.

The fourth chakra is the physical center of our spiritual anatomy and it governs the heart. Our heart's primary task, of course, is to recognize our own spirit in every stranger and to "love our neighbor as ourselves."

We can survive in this world without emotional support, without loving ourselves or other people, but we cannot thrive. The pain of loneliness and isolation has devastating consequences on our emotional and physical health. Most people are afraid of ending up alone, particularly of having to face illness alone—classic fourth-chakra challenges—and thus most people can sense this fear in others.

Fourth-chakra acts of service, more than the other six chakras', illustrate that a 'heartfelt' effort makes a profound difference. They also usually involve a deeper commitment, more of an emotional investment in the act, such as helping someone heal, which can be a long process. The acts of service characteristic of chakras one through three are largely external, such as giving food, clothing, shelter, and money. Acts of devotion and forgiveness are more internal, although their effects also manifest in the physical world. Acts of forgiveness—of welcoming someone back into a circle from which she had been alienated, of bonding with someone in support—are also powerful fourth-chakra gifts.

In performing and receiving some fourth-chakra acts of service, you will undergo a personal transformation. This especially characterizes an act of forgiveness, for instance. Your heart is more open and engaged at this fourth level of consciousness, your intention is stronger, your spirit more willing to stretch past where you once might have been comfortable. You invest your actions with more meaning and are more aware of your own compassion and its purpose.

CHAKRA FIVE, THE ENERGY OF DETERMINATION:

Gifts of Will—Courage and Guidance

The energy associated with your fifth chakra is like a staccato note in music: sharp, intense, transformational. The primary force of this energy center is your will—your sense of determination, purpose, intention, and discipline. This chakra's energy answers the question, "What will I do?" Just as the quality of your life depends upon the quality of choices you make for yourself, the stronger and more determined you are, the better your choices. This is the center of choices and consequences. Located in the throat, this chakra mediates between the head and the heart. It helps us keep our word and fulfill our promises.

We are born with a desire to fulfill our highest potential, purpose, or Sacred Contract, but we do have to *develop* the will to fulfill it. When we are off-track—usually when we are motivated more by fear and expedience than by courage and a vision of what we're meant to do—we become restless and disappointed. Often we need help getting out of such a rut and into the orbit of our highest potential. To be that rocket booster for someone, to catalyze his or her transformation, to have faith in him, to help her generate faith in herself is a great fifth-chakra act of service.

You simply cannot judge the profound impact of your actions—you cannot see the ripples of effects that result from one deed. People who have been key in turning around another person's life often say, "I really didn't do that much for him." Yet the people they have helped always remember them as having altered and improved their life—forever.

CHAKRA SIX, THE ENERGY OF RATIONAL THOUGHT:

Gifts of the Mind—Wisdom and Optimism

Wisdom and optimism are the powers of the sixth chakra, which is located at the center of the forehead. These strengths have a way of showing up together within a person's psyche and soul, the territory of the sixth chakra. It is impossible to be both wise and pessimistic. Yet you have to nurture optimism consciously. "Wisdom arises through effort," Buddha said, and it disappears through lack of effort. You have to *choose* to make the best of a difficult situation and to trust that a reason beyond your understanding is always at work. This is the wisdom to accept things as they are. We gain these powers through living.

"When the student is ready, the teacher appears" is the sixth-chakra adage, and the teacher can be another person, an event, even an illness. The right jewel of wisdom offered at the right time can catch fire in the mind and imagination and allow someone to see a new solution to a problem, a way out of trouble he could not have imagined on his own. Never, ever underestimate the inherent power that exists within your own archive of wisdom, and never judge the quality of your wisdom by the response of the listener. This chakra's gifts are not always recognized immediately by the recipient, who may, however, come to appreciate them later. In sixth-chakra acts of power, the physical world may join forces with consciousness; for instance, you may offer food and a prayer. Keeping an open mind about someone or some situation, staying in the moment and being present for someone are also vitally important sixth-chakra acts of power.

CHAKRA SEVEN, THE CENTER OF HIGHER CONSCIOUSNESS:

Gifts of the Spirit—Angels in Disguise and Good Samaritans

Faith is the power of the seventh chakra, which houses the connection to our own spiritual nature. Seventh-chakra energy governs our capacity to allow our spirituality to become an integral part of our physical lives. It is the circuit to the divine and a porthole to our intuitive resources.

In this domain, miracles abound. You are as likely to be part of a miracle and help it unfold as you are to receive one. The power of faith can take on the physical world and turn dreams into reality, heal illness in the blink of an eye, and make easy everything that was difficult. The acts of service of the seventh chakra include the faith you convey to others through your own beliefs, actions, and prayers. You may also become a human agent in a divine intervention or rescue.

Service to Others Is a Biological Necessity

We must not, in trying to think about how we can make a big difference, ignore the small daily differences we can make which, over time, add up to big differences that we often cannot foresee.

—MARIAN WRIGHT EDELMAN

Being of service is not an option, it is a biological necessity. Every kind action we do for someone is a reanimation of our own life force—and of the other person's. Many spiritual traditions share the Golden Rule: treat others as you would like to be treated.

Each time you reach out to another person, whether you decide to do a small favor or because you feel compelled to help, you perform an invisible act of power that has profound healing effects for you both. What might begin as a physical, sympathetic embrace, for example, can become a source of inspiration for that individual that helps her through a time of despair and well beyond. This is reflected in the following letter from Linda: "Nearly thirty years ago, I was a teenage mother, college student, and waitress. I had no outside financial help and was living from paycheck to paycheck. One month I was not able to make enough money to pay the bills. I was so stressed out with no place else to turn except the state welfare office. It was so deeply humiliating. Before that time, I always had found a way to manage. The basic formula for me had been to get another job. This time, I did not know what to do. I remember having tears in my eyes and being glad that my two-year-old did not have to see me beg for money. I also remember what happened next with supreme clarity, even after all these years. The state employee woman behind the desk stood up, walked around her desk, put her arm around me, and said, 'You are what this agency is for. Don't feel bad and believe me, honey, you will pay this money back tenfold in taxes someday.' She was right and I will never forget her kindness. I am now an attorney with plenty of money, and I enjoy doing small seemingly unnoticed acts of service for people who look like they need someone to talk to."

We respond to someone in need because we see his pain or distress, and we also feel and intuit it through our energy system. Our seven chakras are extremely sensitive to the energy field of every person with whom we come in contact. You may not be consciously evaluating another individual's energy system, but you will pick up on a child's fatigue, a parent's worries, a spouse's stress, or a colleague's disappointment. You don't make it a habit of reading someone's entire chakra system before you say a kind word—you function from a compassionate instinct, an automatic response that kicks in without conscious thought. Choosing *not* to respond to someone is far more conscious, in fact, than reaching out to him.

If you find yourself balking as you begin to help someone, check in with your energy centers to see what's holding you back. The letters I received from people who bypassed opportunities to help another person clearly retain traces of regret. Many people who have turned away from someone in need feel that their own life could have been far better if they had chosen to act more compassionately. We probably are placed in someone's path for a reason—for the opportunity to do good and to fulfill a portion of our life purpose.

Sharla's letter expresses this concern perfectly: "I work with delinquent kids and I still regret a time when I should have hugged one of them. I have worked with kids for more than twelve years and I'm good at it. Some just touch your heart more than others and Oscar was one of those. He was a great kid. He was special. I worry about professionalism and am always careful not to cross any physical boundaries with kids. On Oscar's last day of working with me, he made a motion to hug me. I didn't reciprocate so he backed off. I regret that, still. I don't know if it made a huge difference in Oscar's life that I didn't show him my feelings, but it may have. It was a wonderful opportunity to show him how much he meant to me, and I passed. I wouldn't make that mistake again."

Our intuition senses when someone genuinely needs help. Cathy W. wrote: "I had an unexpected attack of vertigo coming home from a trip and the taxi driver took me straight to the hospital—he made the decision that I was incapacitated. Later he called to see if I was okay. I've never seen him since but I will

always remember his kindness." She feels that the cab driver
saved her life. He could have just driven her home and not paid
much attention to yet another passenger in his cab, but something deep within him responded to her. That wasn't just a ride
to the hospital; it was an invisible act of power in which a human
angel intuitively responded to another person's energy crisis.

The Mystical Nature of Service

The virtue of the universe is wholeness. It regards all things as equal.
— Tao Te Ching

Service to others is not only a social ideal, it is a spiritual ideal
and a spiritual necessity. Virtually all world spiritual traditions
tell us that we serve the divine through caring for other people.
You cannot isolate yourself and evolve in spiritual awareness.
The Talmud states, "All men are responsible for each other."
And Jesus taught, "That which you do to the least of these my
brethren you do unto me."

Folklore and fairy tales are also filled with lessons about the
values of love, compassion, generosity, and caring for family,
friends, the sick, and the elderly. These are the virtues that matter to heaven. These are the virtues that matter even if there is no
heaven. And these are the virtues we are required to develop and
refine on our spiritual journey.

Classic mystical teachings remind us that the process of enlightenment unfolds for each of us on a path that we walk alone.
On that path, everyone we encounter matters. The hungry fellow traveler may be an angel in disguise, testing your virtuous
nature. In folk stories, the generous of heart are rewarded hand-
somely and the selfish suffer nasty consequences that can include
the loss of all earthly possessions, including love. The message is

that we are spiritually responsible for each other and we are meant to discover and nurture the divine that exists within each person.

The message is also that the gods or heaven or the universe observes our actions and records and rewards them. In the Bhagavad Gita, Lord Krishna tells the hero, Arjuna, "Engage yourself in selfless service of all around you, / For selfless service can lead you at last to me." The Qur'an also emphasizes that heaven observes how we distribute our wealth and weighs how we will be blessed:

> A kindly word and a forgiving attitude are better than a charitable action which brings hurt in its train . . . Do not nullify your charitable deeds by posing as munificent or by painfully embarrassing others, as do those people who expend their wealth just to be seen of men, with no faith in God and the last Day. These are to be likened to a nearly bare rock whose scanty soil is left quite denuded after a storm of driving rain. Such people derive no profit at all from their amassings.

Compare this with Jesus' directions:

> Be careful not to parade your uprightness in public to attract attention; otherwise you will lose all reward from your Father in heaven. So when you give alms, do not have it trumpeted before you; this is what the hypocrites do in the synagogues and in the streets to win human admiration. In truth I tell you, they have had their reward. But when you give alms, your left hand must not know what your right is doing; your almsgiving must be secret, and your Father who sees all that is done in secret will reward you.

—MATT. 6:1–4

Similar theologies of service to others are found in Judaism, Buddhism, Taoism, and Native American wisdom, each noting that our behavior is registered by a force greater than our own. Buddhism and Catholicism are known for their rich history of saints, bodhisattvas, and mystics, many of whom attained their iconic status by their service to humanity. Mother Teresa's work with the poor, destitute, and dying in India, for instance, earned her the world's respect and gratitude as well as the Nobel Peace Prize in 1979. She once said, "The biggest disease today is . . . the feeling of being unwanted, uncared for and deserted by everybody. The greatest evil is the lack of love and charity, the terrible indifference toward one's neighbor who lives at the roadside, assaulted by exploitation, corruption, poverty and disease." Evil happens, as it has often been stated, because good people do nothing, and the Buddha cautioned us not to underestimate evil, thinking it will not affect us: "Dripping water can fill a pitcher, drop by drop; one can become filled with evil, even if one accumulates it little by little."

Few people, of course, have the drive to live as Mother Teresa did, and I doubt that even the heavens expect many of us to be called to such devotion. But just a few of these rare individuals—these saints—make us examine our own reaction to people who need help and so also to examine our personal values and actions.

Of the lineage of saints who combined a mystical vision of the oneness of all souls with a practice of service, another St. Teresa—Teresa of Ávila (1515–82) was also famous during her own time. In her most well-known writing, "The Interior Castle," Teresa describes the stages of a soul's awakening by envisioning it progressing through many mansions, each containing many rooms. Each mansion represented a higher level of consciousness of our divine nature and our connection with God,

and one ascends into the mansions through prayer and conscious
inner work. Teresa notes seven interior planes of prayer, which
roughly correspond to the seven chakras, the fifth of which is
particularly significant to us: the fifth mansion symbolizes the
stage of surrender, when we choose to adhere to personal or divine will—it is the wisdom of acceptance. (Acceptance is also the
challenge inherent to the fifth chakra.) We need to accept ourselves, our own power, our need to develop our own power, and
our responsibility to use our power and intuitive guidance in service to others and to the divine.

Here Teresa explains why we need to love and care for
others:

> The Lord asks only two things of us: love for [God] and love
> for our neighbor. . . . The surest sign that we are keeping these
> two commandments is, I think, that we should really be loving
> our neighbor; for we cannot be sure if we are loving God, al-
> though we may have good reasons for believing that we are,
> but we can know quite well if we are loving our neighbor. And
> be certain that, the farther advanced you find you are in this,
> the greater the love you will have for God; for so dearly does
> [God] love us that He will reward our love for our neighbor by
> increasing the love which we bear to Himself and that in a
> thousand ways.

Her message that an individual and God are united through
acts of service is clear.

> What the Lord desires is works. If you see a sick woman to
> whom you can give some help, never be affected by the fear
> that your devotion will suffer, but take pity on her; if she is in
> pain, you should feel pain, too; if necessary, fast so that she may

have your food, not so much for her sake as because you know
it to be your Lord's will. That is true union with His will.

To Teresa, the need to love one's neighbor is a "mystical
love," a transpersonal connection to the divine aspect within
each person. In connecting to the divine in others, we connect to
God. The Hindus also saw the divine nature in man, both tran-
sient and eternal. Other Catholic mystics and saints, such as Ig-
natius Loyola and Thomas Merton, wrote extensively about
finding God through the conscious deepening of caring toward
others, and Teihard de Chardin wrote of the mystical union of
all souls.

Our actions—our works—are an expression of our faith—
our belief in goodness—and an expression of love. When a Buddhist helps the sick or the wounded, it is as if he is serving the
Buddha himself, who represents of all humanity. The bodhisattvas are often depicted as looking over their shoulder at the
viewer, as if encouraging us to follow their lead. And the New
Testament famously says, "God loves a cheerful giver. And God
is able to make all grace abound to you, so that in all things at
all times, having all that you need, you will abound in every
good work."

Mystics and saints maintain a consciousness about the presence of God within themselves and others. They aim to practice
this mindfulness at every moment—at prayer, at work, when
dealing with each other. Out of this practice of noticing, of awakening to who is around us and what is around us, out of this
mindfulness of ourselves and others, we create invisible acts of
power.

From Visible to Invisible Power

Generosity brings happiness at every stage of its expression.
We experience joy in forming the intention to be generous.
We experience joy in the actual act of giving something. And we
experience joy in remembering the fact that we have given.

— THE BUDDHA

I've had four major "aha" experiences—or epiphanies—in my life. One of them in particular profoundly affected my view of the nature of power. On the day I got that insight, I was teaching a workshop to an unusually small gathering of people, which I liked because I would get to know each participant. I was working on new material and enjoying the process of sharing the information and listening to feedback in this intimate setting. But within the first hour of our time together, I sensed something odd in the atmosphere, and by midmorning, everyone was in that restless, distracted funk that usually kicks in only around midafternoon. I suggested that we take a break to wake ourselves up, but even after a brisk walk, within a half hour the group again had settled back into a heavy mood.

During lunch, one of the students, a middle-aged man, asked if he could discuss a personal problem with me. As soon as we were alone, he said, "Nothing in my life ever works. I'm no good at relationships. I don't like my job. I don't have many friends. Can you tell me what my life purpose is? I'm sure if I knew that, I'd be happy."

Usually when someone asks me for help, even if I can't provide an answer, I immediately pick up on his energy and am flooded with images from his past and present. These images can often help the person find an answer. But this time I felt nothing. In fact, the "nothing" took on a heavy, dense, thick something—a fog—that almost put me to sleep. I struggled against this smothering cloud, but my mind was uncharacteristically blank and I finally admitted, "I have no idea what to say to you, and I can't figure out why." He responded, "Figures. No one can help me." Still trying, I asked him questions about his life and each time he answered with one word.

"Do you do anything special with your free time?"

"No."

"Is there another job that you would like to explore?"

"No."

"Is there anything you haven't followed up on in your past that you wish you could do now?"

"No."

"Do you have a particular kind of friend you're looking for?"

"No."

This went on for about five minutes, after which I said, "Well, that's all I can think of to ask you. I'm sorry." As I walked away, I noticed that I felt better and better the farther I got from him. The sensation of dense psychic weight lifted completely as soon as I was in the next room, which is when I suddenly realized that this man had absolutely no conscious base of power. He was psychically, emotionally, mentally, and spiritually depleted. It was his energy—or the palpable lack of it—that had blanketed the classroom with its oppressively sleepy, unconscious atmosphere—not through any malevolence on his part, of course, but as a natural consequence of his lack of life force.

I thought about this poor man long after the workshop had ended because I had rarely encountered a person with such a vacuum in place of an energy field. I kept wondering how he had gotten that way when, suddenly, one day I "downloaded" the answer. An image of the yellow brick road from the film *The Wizard of Oz* snapped into my mind, and I saw that each of us is meant to follow a particular path that reveals itself to us. We are meant to treat our life as a journey, and at each step on that journey, we are meant to notice what is around us and act on opportunities that present themselves. How we act—the decisions and choices we make when we face opportunities or challenges—helps us develop inner strength. This is how we become empowered human beings. If we ignore everything around us, if we cover over our senses with a cloud of indifference, we'll miss the coincidences and synchronicities that signal where we are to go and what we are to do. We have to recognize, accept, and respond gratefully to these synchronicities. Becoming conscious of help that we are offered and willing to use it increases our power.

The man I had met showed all the earmarks of having been unconscious of any attempts by the universe to get his attention and he seemed defeated by the decisions he had made. Yet the consequences for his powerlessness were not only physical and emotional for him—they were also cosmic. They affected everyone around him.

It seems that the universe paces our empowerment to the speed of our willingness to act on our own empowerment—when the student is willing the teacher appears. But we are required to *notice* the teacher, the sign, to hear and heed the call or the signal. Ironically, this man whom I could not help actually performed an act of service for me: he catalyzed my own epiphany and impassioned me to teach people to understand and interpret their life experiences through the lens of power.

The Lens of Power

By cultivating one's nature one will return to virtue.

— CHUANG-TZU

Power has endless forms. But the difference between a visible and invisible act of power cannot be tracked on a scale of good-better-best or small-medium-large. Everything we do for someone else, or he for us, is ultimately empowering or disempowering. We know this instinctively. Everything you think, say, or do in some way influences your physical, emotional, mental, and psychic environment. Think of a how a conversation can leave you feeling wonderful or gutted—words, too, are expressions of power that can have profound effects. Even when a person is seeking affection or a simple compliment, he is seeking empowerment, an infusion of the energy of self-esteem.

Yet many people fear the empowerment of others and do not encourage them, or build their self-esteem, or acknowledge their talent or creativity, or respect their opinions. These people would much prefer to help another person by donating food or money—without becoming involved personally in his or her life—because impersonal involvement is less threatening to their sense of identity and power. The path to your own empowerment is the same as the path to spiritual maturity. It is movement through your first cravings of visible, physical symbols of power (money, property), to your discovery of material things' inability to give you real, inner power, to your development of invisible, higher expressions of power. As you go along this journey, you learn about giving and sharing power, beginning with the visible forms of power in the form of material goods and discovering the invisible powers of love, intuition, compassion, purpose, and spiritual support.

Every action is an exchange of power between two people, no matter if that action is altruistic or acquisitive. Power is the fundamental ingredient of the human experience. I once was part of a conversation between a mother and daughter in which it was painfully obvious that the daughter was striving for her mother's approval—an essential first-chakra energy for building self-esteem. Yet no matter what the daughter said, her mother responded with a nasty, negative comment. Finally, I cornered the mother away from her daughter and asked, "What is wrong with you? Why are you so unkind to your own daughter?" Amazingly enough, this woman gave me an honest answer and said, "Judgment is the only power I have over my daughter." This mother could not bear the very idea of empowering this young girl. She was very generous with clothes and other personal items, but she could not give her daughter the basic acceptance that the girl needed.

In every moment that goes by, some lesson or insight regarding the right use of our power is available, if only we choose to see it. I love the following letter, because this writer completely captures the journey through the limitations of physical power and into the potent nature of spiritual power. Writes Nancy W.: "About God: I thought that God had forgotten me. There is big stuff going on in the world and my little middle-class life in the richest country in the world must not be on his short to-do list. No help from my former husband, constant issues with my son, and minor 'mouth' issues with my other two teenagers. No boyfriend-love to be my companion and let me talk out the issues. Family far away and not able to help. A job that I can do and it's okay, but I have prayed and quit two times hoping to find my writing/consulting job—and nothing.

"Where, indeed, is God? Is every prayer answered? *Yes!* I found him. He is in my ability to move through each day with grace and greet others with genuine interest and care, not feeling ashamed of my life. He is present in my having found a solid yoga practice. He is present in my friendships, running buddies, walking buddies, visiting buddies. He is the reason I don't take Zoloft. He lets me feel the sadness, the fear, and the joy. He is present in Keb' Mo' songs, Stevie Wonder, Van Morrison, Harvey Reid, and Kim Robertson. This is it—this is my life."

Sacred texts describe what is good and bad behavior—or, acceptable and unacceptable uses of our power. Yet in spite of their clear guidance, and in spite of the direct teachings of the world's spiritual leaders, we have also developed many myths about power.

FIRST POWER MYTH:

Life is a battle between the "haves" and the "have-nots." There Is Not Enough to Go Around

Stories in sacred texts from around the world tell us that worrying about not having enough is futile. For example, the Tao Te Ching records that, "The Tao is like a well: used but never used up . . . empty yet infinitely capable. The more you use it, the more it produces." And in one of the greatest teachings of Jesus, he assures us that heaven knows what we need and will provide it.

> Behold the fowls of the air: for they sow not, neither do they reap, nor gather into barns; yet your heavenly Father feedeth them. . . . Take no thought, saying, What shall we eat? or, What shall we drink? or, Wherewithal shall we be clothed? . . .

For your heavenly Father knoweth that ye have need of all these things . . .

But seek ye first the kingdom of God, and his righteousness; and all these things shall be added unto you.

—MATT. 6

Fear of not having enough reveals a lack of faith in our life purpose and in the invisible power that surrounds and supports us. When we look at the disparities of wealth around the world, however, it is easy to become fearful. This mind-set that there is not enough is ingrained deeply in the collective human psyche and it often unconsciously influences our choices and decisions.

How often you have relied upon the following equation when you make decisions: "If I help her or him (with money or praise or effort), that means there will be less (money, happiness, success) for me"? Have you ever decided not to help someone because you thought, "He has enough already"? Have you ever feared that by helping someone, you would help her change from being a "have-not" to a "have"—and your own prosperity or position would suffer? Take your time in answering this last question. Helping someone to become a "have" intimidates a great many people precisely because they are afraid that their own power will be diminished when others' increases. Even though there's no such correlation, that doesn't mean we don't believe it . . . even a bit.

The truth is that the more you empower others, the more powerful *you* become.

SECOND POWER MYTH:

When You Empower Someone Else, You Give Him or Her Power *Over* You

We first associate power with material things, because power over food, shelter, clothing, and money enables us to survive physically. We also associate material rewards and money with power because these enable us to control the events and people in our lives—to a limited extent. We are so terrified of our lives spinning out of control and often feel so vulnerable that we try to shore up our own assets to protect ourselves from other people's material and psychological power plays.

The truth is, the more nonmaterial assets you give someone, the more powerful you become. Measure your generosity toward others not by how much you give, but why you give. Ten dollars given with the sincere hope that it will somehow lift a person's spirits is more effective than one hundred dollars given out of guilt or resentment. Hope—what you intend—is a virtue defined as the desire and search for a future good. Virtue is difficult but not impossible to attain with God's help, however, so your intention is extremely important.

THIRD POWER MYTH:

Material Power Guarantees Happiness

Even though we know that money can't buy us love, the attraction to material power and money can eclipse our reason. Certainly we enjoy life more fully when we do not have to scrape together the bare necessities on a daily basis—that's obvious. But we can't stop ourselves from thinking that we had better guard what we have and always try to get more.

The truth is, inner power is always stronger than material power.

These three myths influence the way almost everyone decides whom to help and how to help them. Even if you are comfortable financially or have already moved beyond material to spiritual concerns, I can guarantee that you once subscribed to these beliefs about power.

Your Survival Instinct: The First, Second, and Third Chakras

Politeness serves a purpose . . . civility and kindness are moral imperatives.

—JANE AUSTEN

Imagine that an hourglass symbolizes your energy anatomy system. The bottom half of the hourglass represents your basic physical identity and houses your first, second, and third chakras. The circumference of the bottom of the hourglass marks the domain of your physical world, your family or community—your "tribe." This is also the energetic territory of your relationships, all your possessions, and everything that you believe affects your survival, such as money and privilege.

The first three chakras give rise to an intuitive sense and gut instinct for what we must do to protect ourselves and our things—family, home, our position in the community, money and belongings. I call these instincts our survival intuition. This instinct even influences how we learn to distinguish right from wrong. According to most social order or tribal law, a person is judged to be either good or bad, an act is right or wrong. We absorb this tribal scale of judgment as we grow up within a society and tend to make automatic decisions according to it. To give you an example of how we do this, for instance, one day as I walked with a male acquaintance through an urban park, we were approached by a homeless person who asked for money. My companion's response was, "Why don't you just get a job?" Even without learning the facts of this homeless man's life, he had judged the man guilty of laziness, as if begging on the street were easy. When I remonstrated with my friend, pointing out that circumstances beyond the man's control might have gotten him fired and homeless, he shrugged and said, "Everyone can find a job. He probably wants money for drugs."

My acquaintance was speaking in the judgemental voice of the tribe; he had concluded that this man obviously must have done something wrong somewhere along the line or he would not be homeless. He must be "bad" because he was guilty of the crime of failing at basic survival. This cut-and-dried position actually revealed my friend's own deep-seated fears about his own survival. He believed that if you do everything right, bad things will not happen to you: If you are a good person, you will never be homeless. If you are a good person, nothing bad will ever happen to you because you do nothing to deserve something bad. My friend had to see the homeless person as someone who had screwed up, or was lazy or weak, or his entire view of how the world works would have come tumbling down. If he had looked at this homeless man compassionately, he would have had to dismantle his entire reality, including his personal theology and belief in a God of order, fairness, and logic

On the other hand, this next story is about just happening to notice something that later you come to believe you were meant to see. Writes Valerie H. "Over the past couple of months, I have been involved in the life of a teenage girl who used to go out with my son. While they were dating, she was tossed out of her dad's house, went back to her mother's, and when she turned sixteen, her mother's boyfriend insisted that she leave. This girl survived a few months at her aunt's house and then I learned that she was in a teen shelter where things had been very difficult for her. I felt a strong impulse to help her and have spent time talking to her, visiting social workers, and generally acting as her champion and advocate. I really could have ignored her situation, but all my 'mother alarm bells' were ringing and I felt a strong protective instinct toward this vulnerable girl. It feels as if this young human being has moved through my sphere and I had to help her."

Our ideas about our place in the world and the workforce are greatly influenced by the general attitudes of our society, which I call the tribal mind. In this mind-set, we identify most strongly with members of our family, ethnic group, religion, and nation. The benefits of belonging to a tribe—the sense of identity we derive, the security and order—can easily become detractions when they are magnified and turn into rigidity, conformity, patriarchy, and xenophobia. Of course, the truth is that any good, hardworking person might suffer enough misfortunes to become jobless or homeless someday. We have to examine any biases we might have and run them through the heart chakra—the gateway to the higher chakras and powers—which lies in the neck of the hourglass. But first, let's get some perspective on the higher chakras and the dynamics of their very different energies.

The View from Above: The Fifth, Sixth, and Seventh Chakras

In the top half of the hourglass are the fifth, sixth, and seventh chakras. These three energy centers are aligned to our internal, higher powers. The higher consciousness of the upper chakras transcends the territorial values of the lower chakras and helps us move beyond the tribal, earthbound way of thinking. The higher chakras' enegies have the potential to help us become free from fear and allow us to see our unlimited potential. Through the constant flow of energy between the lower and higher chakras, and through living in the physical world and nurturing awareness of the spiritual, visible power grows into greater, invisible power. The energy of the higher chakras also motivates us to move from individual, self-referential ways of seeing the events in our lives to looking beyond the details to a greater, symbolic meaning.

Through my years of work as a medical intuitive, I have seen many people who hold onto past injuries and emotional pain to the detriment of their health and their lives. They can and do spend years asking a question that has no real answer, "Why did this happen to me?" It is impossible to heal from those injuries through logical discussions or by rehashing details to try to find blame. I have never once seen blame enhance someone's healing. But the decision to seek a greater purpose above and beyond the personal situation and pain is very healing.

Say, for instance, that you had a terrible relationship with a parent or sibling when you were young, which is very common, as is carrying resentment or angry memories about it. Instead of miring yourself in the negative energy and details of old jealousies or disappointments, however, take a step back and look objectively at the entire canvas of your life. Did your dealing with that difficult emotional situation prepare you to face later challenges? Find ways to appreciate your experiences, especially the difficult ones. To get to that point of appreciation, you have to muster the will and courage to face any pride and anger that you feel, which have a way of keeping you stuck in your own sense of self-righteousness. But being right when it means being angry and unhappy serves no one, least of all you. Get beyond that.

Everything's got a moral, if only you can find it.

—LEWIS CARROLL

When you widen your perspective into a bigger picture and pick out the definite patterns and themes, you're using what I call symbolic sight. This bigger, better perspective helps you see the kinds of challenges that recur in your life that you are meant to face and the strengths that you are meant to develop. Are there recurring patterns of behavior and events, any coincidences or signposts—evidence of grace—that may indicate where you are going and what you are meant to do? Many of the people who wrote the letters in this book survived their difficulties precisely because they discovered the grace of purpose at work in their lives.

Every time we encounter someone, we unconsciously make either a compassionate or judgmental response. We may respond with fear—based on a false belief about power—or feel personally intimidated or we respond with compassion—our higher consciousness. If you pause in moments when you are conflicted, you will intuitively sense how to shift your reaction.

Maeve wrote of her regret for not having acted to help someone in need: "One night I was out with two friends and stopped by a take-out place for some food. I didn't eat any of it, intending to take it home. As we were walking away from the restaurant, I was stopped by a man who asked me if I was carrying food and if he could have it. He asked me three times. I said no each time, as this meal was something special that I knew I wouldn't get for a while. When I got home that evening, I opened the food container only to discover that it had turned sour and I had to throw it away. I will never forget that hungry man."

What makes us shun a hungry person or beggar or recognize that "There but for the grace of God go I"? Sometimes we look the other way because we so fear that the person's circumstances could visit us as well. Our survival instincts make us want to get away as fast as we can, but our interior voice often directs us to face this reality and need. Maeve's interior voice in fact told her she should have given the man her meal. Ours often compels us to act compassionately—outside the boundaries of our normal patterns of self-protection and fear.

Sometimes, however, our inner voice will direct us to say no to another person, to walk away when asked for help, and to protect ourselves. I was having lunch with a friend when two kids walked into the restaurant and asked us for directions. My instincts told me that these two were con artists, but my mind said they looked far too innocent. They said that they were lost and trying to get to their aunt's home, a story that made me think that they were sweet boys, even though I still had a bad gut feeling about them. By the time they finished their hard-luck story—and the lunch we had bought them—we were practically hiring a limo to make sure they arrived at their aunt's home safely. After thanking us for lunch and directions, they left the restaurant—and took with them my friend's purse, which they had managed to steal somewhere between lunch and a quick farewell. If your gut urges you to help and your mind tries to stop you, check in with your heart. If your gut tells you to protect yourself, listen to it.

When you are asked to help, ask yourself, "Why me? Why do I think that man chose to reach out to me?" When I've asked my students this, their answers have ranged from, "I'm an easy mark," and "They can tell I won't say no," to "God meant for me to help." Intuition directs people *to* those who can help them. Whether someone asks directly for your help or you "just happen to notice" another person looking lost or injured, your intuition is resonating with the signals from that other energy field. We use our gut instincts whenever we reach out to help friends or strangers and when we ask for help from them.

Because we are all united by a common energy field, we become more attuned to others' energy systems, regardless of whether they are friend, family, or stranger. We understand wholly that the physical and temporal boundaries and distinctions of space, culture, religion, and ethnic heritage that separate us are illusions. Once we have recognized this great truth, that all are one, our intuition calls us to act in even bolder ways than we would previously have considered.

Cheryl wrote of one such experience: "I am usually very hesitant about stopping or picking someone up on the side of the road. However, as I was driving to work one day I saw a woman walking and a car on the side of the road with a flat tire. Initially I passed her by and took my usual exit. Yet something inside told me that I couldn't just go to work and sit at my desk. I turned around, went back, and asked the woman if she needed assistance or a ride. She asked if I could bring her to where she could make a phone call, so I drove her to a nearby restaurant. I also asked if she needed change to call, which she did. About two weeks later, as I was leaving the grocery store, I met that lady again, with her ten-year-old daughter. She came over and introduced me to her daughter, adding that I was the person who assisted her when she was in trouble. She told her daughter, 'You see, there are still good people in the world.' I never saw her again and the only thing I can say is there was something from deep inside of me that told me I could not leave that person on the side of the road. I am grateful I listened."

Ordinary thinking would maintain that it was a coincidence that these two women saw each other again, but you know better. To learn that there are still good people in the world could well be a soul lesson for the child. Who knows how many others in this world will benefit from one young girl believing in the goodness of life? If that isn't an invisible act of power and healing cleverly disguised as a flat tire, then I don't know what is. Synchronistic encounters are meaningful; they are manifestations of an invisible power working with you and through you.

*   *   *

A human being is a part of a whole, called by us universe, a part
limited in time and space. He experiences himself, his thoughts and
feelings as something separated from the rest . . . a kind of optical
delusion of his consciousness. This delusion is a kind of prison for us,
restricting us to our personal desires and to affection for a few persons
nearest to us. Our task must be to free ourselves from this prison by
widening our circle of compassion to embrace all living creatures and
the whole of nature in its beauty.

—ALBERT EINSTEIN

Science and religion tell us that we are energetically interdependent; that matter and energy are the same throughout the universe. Our spiritual interconnectedness and intuitive signals form, in effect, an energetic Internet. Extraordinary circumstances often connect us to people we may not physically meet for many years.

This next letter tells a remarkable story of a connection that was obviously meant to be, even though its beginning was rooted in tragedy. Writes Christine P.: "In 1977, when I was just starting college, I fell in love for the first time with a ski instructor who I met at a resort. We loved one another a great deal. He lived in Northern California and I lived in Los Angeles. Months later, during midsemester break, I had an urge to visit him and convinced a girlfriend to drive with me. The visit was wonderful. I felt special, loved, and hopeful for this budding relationship. But it was not meant to be.

"Three hours into our ride back home, my friend and I found ourselves in the midst of a downpour of rain, a heavy fog, and dangerous driving conditions. We pulled over to wait out the storm. My friend then shared with me that she had a bad feeling in the pit of her stomach that something wasn't right. This was around 10 P.M. We arrived safely home around midnight. I decided to stay overnight at her place because I was exhausted from the drive.

"The next morning, I received a phone call from a close acquaintance of my boyfriend's, telling me that my boyfriend and some of his buddies had driven into a local resort town to have a few drinks. On the return home, the designated driver was driving my boyfriend's jeep, lost control, and drove it off the road, down a steep, forested embankment toward a stream. All the passengers were thrown from the jeep, including my boyfriend, who landed in the spot where the jeep rolled right on top of him, ending his life. The others had only a few bruises and scratches.

"My heart filled with a pain that I had never before experienced. The healing process was slow and difficult and I wondered if the hurt would ever stop. During this period, I read all his letters to me, looked at photographs of the two of us together, and kept remembering all the good times we'd had. It occurred to me then that I should send some photographs to his parents, who lived in Illinois. I had never met them, but found their address and wrote a heartfelt letter with the photographs. A bond developed between my boyfriend's mother and me as a result of our mutual loss that has blossomed into a twenty-six-year-long deep and lasting friendship. Twenty years after his death, along with countless letters, gifts, phone calls, and support during my ten-year marriage and divorce, I finally visited his mother for the first time. I had to drive three hours from the Chicago airport to a small, quiet farm community. I arrived at a house with balloons streaming from the front door and a sweet little lady came to greet me with open arms. Our time was so special together and I knew this friendship was meant to be. We have bonded like mother and daughter. His two sisters and their families have also opened their homes to me.

"God closes one chapter, he begins anew with the next— a blueprint of love and compassion wherein we create our own unique details. The death of my first love was not in vain and I am reminded daily that God's ways of giving are amazingly simple but always so powerful. For any of us who look for substance in material things, we are sure to miss most of God's daily gifts to us."

The Great Mediator: The Fourth Chakra

Pure spirit reaches in the four directions, flows now this way, now that—there is no place it does not extend to. Above, it brushes heaven; below, it coils on the earth. . . . Its name is called One-with-Heaven. . . . Guard the spirit . . . and you will become one with spirit, . . . which communicates and mingles with the Heavenly Order.

—CHUANG-TZU

In the center of the hourglass is your fourth energy center, your heart chakra, the funnel between the bottom and the top of the hourglass. Here the domains of your ego *and* your spirit meet. The fourth chakra is the seat of the energy of compassion, which bridges the differences between people. In this center of emotional perceptions, the heart softens the mind's strict judgments. Without the heart's influence, the mind can become defensive, hard, brittle, uncompromising, and cold. It can also lack discernment, stamina, or principles. The fourth chakra is "central control"; it mediates between mind and body. When the heart is engaged, it drives the body to act on the mind's ideas; when your heart energy is absent—when your heart is not in something, your actions have no force.

When sympathy pierces your heart, your entire being responds. Your mind rushes to the front with ideas and solutions but it also may raise fears and assumptions to prevent a heart connection. Just as Maeve's heart was opening to the homeless man, for example, her mind allowed her to say no to his request for food. The heart's response is so powerful, however, that Maeve still remembers it—her heart won't let her mind forget.

The challenge that we all face is to ask the authority of the mind to work *with* the compassion of the heart, to become congruent. When our upper chakras operate congruently, inspiration, strength, drive, commitment, and faith all rush directly into our biology. This spiritual clarity allows the sands from the top of the hourglass to flow freely into the bottom, uniting mind and body, compassion and action.

When mind and heart are congruent, you act confidently, fearlessly, and make good choices in managing your physical power. You achieve the goal of spiritual transformation: to function compassionately and consciously as you move from thought into form.

A congruent person can afford to empower others. A person who lacks a sense of congruency might muster up enough pity or charity to buy a fish for a hungry person, but for him to teach that person to fish would seem threatening to his own power—he would fear that the person would learn to fish better than he and would outperform him. As a man at one of my workshops told me, "I would give my friend a thousand dollars to help him and his family get by, but I would not give him a thousand dollars to start a business—and pass me by."

How do you become congruent? How do you unite the information from your survival intuition with the guidance from your higher consciousness? How do you become so empowered that helping others does not threaten your own sense of security? In the next chapters, we will explore these and other worthy questions and help you examine your own spirit and purpose.

> *Service is the rent we pay to be living. It is the very purpose of life and not something you do in your spare time.*
>
> —MARIAN WRIGHT EDELMAN

And as for You . . .

Next time someone offers you help, check out what that does for your biology. When someone refuses to help you, see how that feels, too. Note specifically where your body responds, because the offer or refusal will find its chakra base. Note if your gut clenches, or your anger flushes hot, or a tension headache kicks in. Also note how much you rely upon your nonverbal means of communicating to others that you need assistance, love, attention, kindness—or perhaps a loan, some companionship, a recommendation for a raise or a promotion. We have become a culture in which words are our last means of communication. Your invisible power and energy are who you are. You have been called to live with this energy and power and use them well.

> PRAYER OF ST. FRANCIS OF ASSISI
> Lord, make me an instrument of thy peace.
> Where there is hatred, let me sow love;
> Where there is injury, pardon;
> Where there is doubt, faith;
> Where there is despair, hope;
> Where there is darkness, light;
> Where there is sadness, joy.
> O divine Master, grant that I may not so much seek
> To be consoled as to console,
> To be understood as to understand,
> To be loved as to love;
> For it is in giving that we receive;
> It is in pardoning that we are pardoned;
> It is in dying to the self that we are born to eternal life.

As you read the following chapters, keep these universal truths in mind:

- You are where you are supposed to be and in every moment there is an opportunity to serve another or to receive support.
- There are no such things as coincidences or accidents. Look for the meaning in your synchronistic encounters.
- Any form of assistance you offer is an act of healing.
- Anything you do for others, as well as the support you receive in your own life, has healing consequences for the whole human community.
- You will always receive help within a second of a prayer. To recognize the help, you must see everything in your life from that second on as a part of the answer to your prayer.
- Everything you do consciously is an invisible act of power.

PART II

The Journey to Empowerment

CHAPTER 1

Gifts of the Earth: The First Chakra

When you pray, do not imitate the hypocrites: they love to say their prayers standing up in the synagogues and at the street corners for people to see them. In truth I tell you, they have had their reward. But when you pray, go to your private room, shut yourself in, and pray to your Father who is in that secret place, and your Father who sees all that is done in secret will reward you.

—MATT. 6:5–6

Whenever we describe the nature of the human experience, we try to surmise the reasons the heavens created all of us in the first place. Why are we here? Where do we come from? Where are we going? Calvin, the child terror/philosopher in the comic strip "Calvin and Hobbes," gives one answer: "Well, I don't know about anyone else, but I came from my room, I'm a kid with big plans, and I'm going outside! See ya later!" I've been looking for more metaphysical answers, however, and over the years I have left at the wayside the explanation I was taught in my Roman Catholic school, "God made us because he loves us." As I learned about the human energy system and its exquisite design, I saw that just as we are both spiritual and physical beings, our purpose in life is both physical and spiritual.

I know that is not the easy answer that many people will like. We would like our answers to be black or white, not both, not gray. We would like to be able to live according to a simple theology—essentially, we want a neat, clear relationship with the heavens in which good behavior is rewarded with wondrous blessings and bad behavior gets its just desserts. But life is just not that simple, although the cosmos does have laws. A part of the cosmic puzzle fell into place for me one day around 1985, when I was doing an intuitive health reading for a woman I will call Joan.

Whenever I conduct a medical intuitive reading, impressions of that person's life and memories, including any unfinished business, flood my vision. But with Joan, I received only one image: I had an overwhelming vision of an enormous tree whose roots were brittle and broken. The tree represented Joan's life, but her spirit was only partially engaged in keeping that tree alive. Her energy did not flow all the way through the trunk to the roots—her first chakra. I felt that Joan lacked any sense of belonging—to her life, her body, or her being—and saw that her spirit was disengaged from her life. She was unmoored, lacking direction; she had no passion or enthusiasm. It seemed as if she were fighting having ever been assigned to her life in the first place, her mind and spirit completely at odds with each other. Her mind mistrusted life and was frightened of it, while her spirit longed to have meaning and purpose. She was disintegrating bit by bit spiritually, emotionally, and physically.

This intuitive reading had a profound effect on me. Along with the powerful image of the enormous spirit tree, I got the distinct sense that the universe is constructed in such a way that there is a place for each of us in it and that we are each meant to find that place as well as "become" that place. And I saw that if we do not try to find that place or purpose, we suffer emotionally and spiritually and, ultimately, physically. This was one of the first inklings I had that before we are born, we commit to a life in this body at this time with these particular circumstances and we commit to learning our spiritual purpose—our Sacred Contract—through our life experiences.

Growing Your Roots

The purpose of life is a life of purpose.

—GEORGE BERNARD SHAW

Our first chakra plants us in the physical, visible world. There is always a tension to living in a physical body. Our mind and spirit are often at odds with each other and we struggle to balance their desires. The spirit within us has faith that our needs will always be met, but our mind perceives that there is not enough to go around. Our spirit inherently understands that we are all one— with other people and our universe—but our mind finds this belief difficult to maintain as we live our daily lives, coming into conflict with loved ones and colleagues. We generally can manage to remember that we are "one" with our spouse or partner or biological family, but it takes a very real leap in our spiritual evolution to be able to see ourselves as one with the rest of humanity and to act in accordance with that insight. Living as we usually do within that gap between our spirit's perception of truth and our mind's perception of reality, however, we learn about energy and power.

All of life's lessons can be summarized in one word: power. Power affects our biology and our spirit. Power can represent people, status, stuff, money, cars, toys, knowledge, skills—anything that enhances our ability to survive in the physical world. Every decision we make, every item of clothing we wear, as well as any burning desire we have—whether that's simply to be at the head of a line or to sit in a corner office—all determine what has power in our lives and what we are willing to do and say in order to get power, use it, and keep it. Each of the chakras provides a different lens through which you see and experience power. And the journey begins at the first chakra, our entry into the physical world.

The goal of the human experience is to transform ourselves from beings who long to attain power in the physical world to beings who are empowered from within. This is the classic hero's quest. You embark on a journey to awaken self-knowledge and inner strength. It may sound simple in theory, but it is brutal in terms of life experience. Think of all the fears and temptations, dragons and physical obstacles that the archetypal hero, the knight or warrior, must overcome and slay before proving himself returning home to court, to his full rightful place in the world. His quest also inevitably includes an encounter that requires his ability to tap into the invisible or spirit world to attain discernment, wisdom, and his full power. Today this archetype of male and female power is seen in the superheroes of comic books and movies, such as Superman and Xena, or *Star Wars* and *Lord of the Rings*.

If there could be a single, universal test of our spirit it would be: do we have faith in our ability to survive in the physical world or are we afraid of the challenges life sets us? Every single challenge in life and every single spiritual crisis tests the quality of our decisions. We want to come to the point where even when our back is against the wall, we can make a conscious choice with integrity. We may be coping with a family problem, or making a financial decision that will affect a personal relationship, or trying to help a stranger. But each test brings our spirit face to face with fears about our own ability to survive. We have to decide, do we turn inward and trust the inherent wisdom of our spirit that reminds us of universal truths such as, "Give and it is returned tenfold unto you" and "Do unto others as you would have them do unto you," or do we cave into insecurities that allow us to turn away?

When you view your life symbolically, as a spiritual journey, it allows you to examine more objectively your actions as well as your decisions not to act. You can attempt to draw a lesson from every encounter and experience. For instance, suffering a betrayal can be emotionally devastating, but it usually teaches us that we have to let go of expectations, of emotional and psychological dependencies and our attempt to control others because of our own fears. It teaches us to accept others as they really are, not as we would wish they were or hoped they would be. It also signifies that we cannot completely control our lives.

Ultimately, to fulfill our purpose, we need to be in certain relationships and go through unpleasant experiences in order to learn to be in better ones. The ending of any relationship necessarily forces you down a new path. Although at first you might fight this new direction, when you finally surrender to it, you will be able to see your new circumstance as a blessing after all. You can choose to view crises as arbitrary and antagonistic or as interventions that are part of a greater plan—signposts that direct you to your next lesson about your own personal power and Sacred Contract.

Of course, you don't have to wait for a crisis to see things symbolically. Your spiritual life is not only about trying to figure out why bad things happen to you or others—or rather, to figure out the meaning of those bad experiences, since we will never understand fully why. You can approach the enjoyable events and patterns in your life as well as any troubles with the intention of seeing a greater purpose hidden within them. For instance, consider why you have a good relationship with certain people or what led you to become involved in an especially rewarding line of work or hobby. You are meant to find the right path to enjoy your life fully, to find meaning in your daily activities and interactions with other people. You can start wherever you are, today. You are meant to "be here now," as Ram Dass has so famously asserted.

Providing assistance is an act of spiritual alchemy in which you transfer energy or grace to someone else. It is actually the electricity of your intention and thoughtfulness that provides the life-transforming energy. People have told me many stories about how they just did the "tiniest" thing for someone who, in return, overwhelmed them with expressions of gratitude. They were mystified by the reaction when they measured it against the size of the favor, at least as they saw it. Yet they had provided an invisible act of empowerment.

I have taught for many years that "Your biography becomes your biology," but now I can add that "What serves the spirit serves the body." All your physical and mental stress is rooted in issues of survival—concerns involving the lower three chakras. Whether it is lower back pain, which often indicates financial stress; or cardiac concerns, which can relate to emotional pressures on the job or at home; or a lack of self-nurturing or care— somewhere in the mix of all the individual details of your life are insecurities regarding survival. It is impossible to be fully healthy while you feel threatened. You could have all the money in the universe and still be so stressed that you would become ill from, for instance, the fear of being alone or abandoned.

True security is a matter of the spirit. You want to learn to see the needs of your spirit as symbols of energy. Therein lies the universal truth that puts us all on an equal footing: each of us must come to discover through our many life experiences whether we have faith in our spiritual purpose, in our very existence, or whether we fear the journey of our life. When fear pervades our being, it lessens our capacity to share or to be compassionate, or even to do the smallest kind favor.

Unconsciously—and sometimes consciously—we find it impossible to help another person if we perceive ourselves as powerless. We cannot, for example, offer someone money for a meal if we fear starvation; we cannot give another person trust in his talents if we fear that he will leave us as a result; and we cannot support someone's success if we believe that it will threaten our own. Even our briefest interactions ultimately come down to how willing we are to share the power of our body, mind, and spirit. In all cases, the equation we use—whether we are kind or judgmental, generous or miserly, patient or abrupt—is based upon a deeply unconscious measuring stick that weighs the exchange of power inherent in each thought, action, and word, regardless of how private or public, grand or subtle. Your relationship to power is always the catalyst for doing something or not.

Let's start examining and building your power at its beginning—in the first chakra.

The Consciousness of Your First Chakra

Every chakra has a key word that characterizes its energy. The first chakra's is *tribe*. This chakra's motto is "We are all one." The first chakra is your connection to your roots, your physical world, your family. It is your basic support system, the energy field that most strongly engages with the basic tasks of life and survival—shelter, food, clothing, work, family, and friends. The first chakra holds the energy of our first consciousness—of ourselves as part of a family. The sacrament of baptism is the sacred rite I associate with the first chakra, which symbolizes our acceptance by our family and our community. The sacraments are based on divine connections. We don't enact them simply because they are social customs. They convey important, universal human values and divine values. They create a divine connection between our consciousness and our souls, between us and other people, and between us and God.

The life task or spiritual challenge of the first chakra is to accept our own physical life in the package it came in and come to see that package as essential to our incarnation and our sacred journey. We "baptize" ourselves, in other words. Each of us will have some "sacred flaw," something given to us to endure— maybe it's a physical condition or a family burden we have to learn to live with—something *we* cannot change but that is meant to make *us* change. Through this sacred flaw we are meant to connect to divine mystery. This mark or burden given to us by the gods at our birth signals us that our life will not unfold in a logical, orderly sequence of right and wrong, good and bad, pain and pleasure. We look for the blessing in the boulder we cannot remove from our path and come to be grateful for our lives, accepting the journey that is ours alone to live. The point at which we stop asking, "Why me?" and accept that some things can never have rational explanations marks the beginning of our acceptance of the spiritual mystery of divine will. In so many of the letters sent me, people cited their moment of letting go of a need to know why they were in a difficult position as starting them on the road to empowerment. The Serenity Prayer at the end of this chapter can guide us in this task: "God grant me the serenity to accept the things I cannot change."

Carol C. wrote, "The most powerful act of service I have ever received was when my sister donated a kidney to me. In the literal sense, she saved my life. From an emotional level, I realized how much love surrounded me and I am still awestruck at how many people prayed for me. From a symbolic level, I understand that this was part of my contract with my sister as well as all the other lives that were touched by my experience. I had to surrender my will to God's will. For me to be so vulnerable and to have to ask for such a sacrifice was like trying to speak a foreign language. The fact that I really didn't have to ask since all my sisters and my husband offered a kidney in order to keep me alive brought me to my knees in gratitude."

The law of energy—like attracts like—rules the greater human community. A man drove up to a gas station and asked the attendant, "What are the people like in this town? I'm thinking of moving and I want to know ahead of time what type of neighbors I can expect." The gas station attendant replied, "Well, what were your neighbors like in the town you're leaving?" The man answered, "They were nasty gossips who never had a good word to say about anyone." "Oh," said the attendant, "you'll find them pretty much the same in this town. I'd recommend you keep on looking for another town." Later a second man pulled into the gas station, asking the same question, "What types of people live in this town?" And again, the gas station attendant inquired, "Well, what types of people live near you now?" "Oh," he said, "they are wonderful, kind people." To which the gas station attendant replied, "You'll find them much the same right here in this town."

The law of attraction, working through your first chakra, attracts to you types of people who reflect your social, moral, political, ethnic, and religious values. Among these values are the attitudes you hold about society and how you view the essential nature of humanity. Are people basically good? Are you available to help others? Can the universe send people to you in need? Can you count on the same should you ever be in need of help? These are first-chakra questions about which you long ago made up your mind—even if you didn't consciously ask yourself how you would answer them. These answers determine how you connect to the energy of people around you, belong to a community, grow roots, and create a home where you are known and loved.

The first chakra symbolizes our individual connection to others, which brings people to our door as friends, neighbors, and miracle workers, as Linda B. discovered when she faced circumstances in her life that could not be changed, but only accepted. She wrote, "My son, who is five years old with type I diabetes, befriended a neighbor boy whose mother took on the task of learning to monitor his blood sugar and deliver insulin via the insulin pump—which is a huge responsibility. She had seen the ambulance in front of our house for an emergency with my son, but she did this so the boys would not always have to play at my house, as is the case with his other friends. Her courage showed my son that there are others who can take care of him and it also gave me a much needed break. By that act, this woman is my friend always."

No man is an island, entire of itself; every man is a piece of the continent.

—JOHN DONNE

Each of the chakras houses a universal truth that pulses steadily within our energy field. The truth that all is one resonates within our first-chakra energy center and makes us consider the question, "How responsible are we for one another?" This is, without a doubt, one of the central philosophical and theological questions of life, not to mention the archetypal issue that guides world events. Exactly how responsible *are* we for one another? Am I my brother's keeper? The question of responsibility can be discussed from a moral perspective as well as an ethical one, but it is essentially an individual spiritual matter. We must each answer that question for ourselves. And we will be asked to answer it again and again, as if we are taking a cosmic exam.

As I watched a television program one night with a friend, a public-service announcement for sending aid to impoverished, hungry children came on the screen. My friend said, "Oh, God, those poor kids. I hope people respond." (She called to contribute later that evening.) Her genuine sympathy was a natural first-chakra response, a recognition of her kinship with others in this world and responsibility to them, which led her to respond to their need for basic assistance.

You need a substantial amount of courage to open wide your first chakra and admit the truth of something that goes against what you've been taught by your family or tribe. If your clan taught you, for instance, that people should take care of themselves, but you believe in helping others, heaven will send you people to serve, and you will need to face the disapproval of your tribe, community, or colleagues. Acknowledging any sense of responsibility for each other is simultaneously an act of spiritual awakening. It also acknowledges the authority of the universe's spiritual laws over physical laws or social obligations.

Even if you do not consciously acknowledge a universal truth, however, it is still going to affect you. You will continually find yourself with opportunities to acknowledge, for instance, that all of us are one until you make it a part of your life creed and act according to its promptings. Once you open to this law, you will notice an intensification of your intuition. You will become more attuned to people with first-chakra concerns and vulnerabilities. You might notice people in need, for example, and act to help them more than you had before, or your negative judgments of people may gradually disappear because you no longer fear them and their circumstances or see their predicaments as "contagious," as many people do.

Obviously, you cannot help everyone, nor are you expected

to. You have to practice discernment even as you listen to your intuition. Many people report that they feel responsible for everyone, which is an exaggerated concern, out of all proportion to our purpose. Before you take on the world, take on your family, your friends, and, as St. Teresa of Ávila recommended, your neighbors—then you know you're serving God. Your intuition and common sense will help show you the way.

Allen M. shared his experience in giving the help he knew he could—and accepting the help he had to—in his letter: "I work as a volunteer one day a week running a small program that distributes clothes to homeless people. Last winter two of my colleagues spent a couple of hours helping me transport five hundred winter coats provided by an outside organization. It was such an extraordinary help. It was a great relief because I had to go through a lengthy process of filing applications [for people] who qualify for receiving the coats and I had no idea how I would transport the coats themselves." Had Allen not accepted help from others in his own mission, he'd still be working on that one task.

Folk stories and legends also advise us to listen to our inner guidance and accept the help offered to us. In *Women Who Run with the Wolves*, Clarissa Pinkola Estés tells the story of the witch Baba Yaga and the orphaned girl Vasalisa, whose dying mother had given her a small magic doll to guide her. When Vasalisa is driven into the wild forest by her evil stepmother and stepsisters, ostensibly to retrieve embers for a fire from Baba Yaga, she relies on the doll's instructions—symbol of her spirit or intuition—to lead her safely along the many dark paths to the witch's house. There, before giving her the fire, Baba Yaga sets many impossible tasks for Vasalisa, including separating one thing from another—sorting mildewed from good corn, poppy seeds from dirt—and answering mysterious questions. The girl is able to do this all by consulting the little doll—or trusting in her innate wisdom and first-chakra intuition, a gift from her mother or tribe. So, too, our intuition guides us through even seemingly impossible tasks and teaches us to make fine distinctions in judgment. We learn to separate old, worn-out tribal beliefs from useful, new ideas, for instance, and nourishing seeds of information from the grit and grime that surrounds us.

The archetypal hero Hercules was assigned twelve seemingly impossible labors. Whenever it seemed that he would not be able to complete a task, the sympathetic deities Hermes (the messenger) and Athena (wisdom)—signifying inner guidance or intuition—would appear. Through his struggles, suffering, and service. Hercules himself became a god, much revered by the ancient Greeks as a model of the virtues of strength, perseverance, and acceptance of his life tasks.

> *I am only one, but still I am one. I cannot do everything, but still I can do something; I will not refuse to do something I can do.*
>
> —HELEN KELLER

The vulnerability of our own spirit inevitably surfaces when we allow ourselves to care for others. Once that place in us is up and running, it is difficult to turn that intuitive sensor off. Allen M. notes, "We have such romantic visions of the saints helping others that we can never imagine Mother Teresa having to make tough choices between helping one person over another. And until we do this work ourselves, we can never imagine that the needy and homeless would be anything but grateful. Yes, it's possible that the spiritual nature of Mother Teresa's very being was so great that it may have melted away any negative feelings [regarding] those she helped. It's more likely that the heavens sent

Mother Teresa very tough choices just like they send the rest of us and at times she may have questioned her own judgments. However, I imagine that it's the very persistence with which she kept choosing to serve selflessly, regardless of the tough choices she may have had to make, that actually purified her spirit."

Janie G. adds her own wisdom to the practice of service, writing, "If everyone thought of how they could be of service when they were able to, the world would be a more peaceful place. I am careful to give only when it is appropriate and not encourage codependence or inappropriate exchanges. And I have developed a good sense for when service is (or is not) appropriate."

Janie G.'s own story is of a classic first-chakra challenge to her survival. She writes, "My husband and I have been together for thirty years. Seven years ago we were having a really hard time and separated to try and get clear. We gave a brief explanation to our oldest kids, aged sixteen and eighteen at the time, and told the younger two, who were eight and ten, that Dad was working a job too far away to live at home. I was working two jobs as well as home schooling the younger children and was pretty overwhelmed. Without asking for help, my oldest two children curtailed their social activities and put in countless hours watching the younger children, cooking, and driving them to their activities. Although they had always been helpful, they were particularly available that entire year without being asked. It touched me so much that they were willing to set aside their young adult social activities to support me that I agreed to try to make things work out with their father. We are now happily together and planning the wedding of my oldest child, who has learned that relationships can survive tough spots with love and support from a family."

Not all forms of assistance or service that we extend to

each other emerge from crises, of course. But in the stories that follow, heaven comes to call just when someone needs it the most.

The Gifts of the Earth

We can survive without an occupation, not well perhaps, but we can, and we can survive without a tribal support system. But we cannot survive without food, shelter, and clothing, the gifts of the earth that are essential for us to function even basically, let alone effectively and optimally, in the physical world. Yet divine provisions are not subject to long-range planning but show up when needed. People describe their rescue as happening, "Just when I had given up hope" or "Out of the blue." We can't decode divine reasoning.

Crises make us focus on the here and now. They bring us into present time. After all, no one tries to process unfinished emotional business from her childhood while looking for a cat in a house fire. When confronted with emergencies, we are more open to outrageous, out-of-character, intuitive guidance because we are in "present time" and often have no choice but to listen to it. In the midst of these in-the-moment challenges, we encounter coincidences and synchronicities. After the dust settles and we have time to review our experience, we might realize that while we have been busying ourselves trying to nail down the floor beneath our first-chakra feet, the heavens have been scheming to get us to look up and beyond these basic concerns. Perhaps the message is that the present will always have more to offer us than our past and crises emerge to make us value our lives in the moment. And sometimes we simply need to move on but have to be made to do so.

The Gift of Shelter

Be our shelter, Lord, *our companion when we are away, and our welcome guest when we return.*

— CATHOLIC HOUSEHOLDS BLESSINGS AND PRAYERS

Connie H. lost everything in a fire. Even though the fire wiped out every piece of her history, however, a compassionate tribe made certain that she would have a future. "When I arrived at the scene, my house was surrounded by fire trucks, people I knew, and people I did not know. My older daughter shouted, 'Mom, don't go near the house, stay away,' but I went toward the door, took one step in, and passed out from the heat. When I opened my eyes, my younger daughter was standing over me, saying, 'It's going to be okay, Mommy, it's going to be okay.' All the voices around me were correct in what they were saying; I could not do anything to help. I did not have anyplace to sleep, everything I owned was gone. Within the next hour, a truck pulled up hauling a trailer. Family and people I did not know hooked it up to water and electricity at nearby homes. Food and more people came, about twenty family members and neighbors I had never met . . . along with ribs, pizza, and drinks.

"My two dogs had been saved by a team of satellite TV in-stallers. My cat was shooed out the door by firemen, but now she was missing. About ten neighborhood children formed a huge chain and began to search the field for her. I did not know any of them and they did not know my cat . . . and the last thing she would do is come to the call of, 'Here, kitty-kitty.' Soon it was dark and only my family was left. My son-in-law and daughter led me to bed in my trailer, so that I could stay near the remains of my home. All of a sudden we heard a faint meow. I followed it and found my cat under the woodpile next door, totally covered in soot, including around her nostrils. I scooped her up, took her into my trailer, and went to bed, holding her all night. Over the next three days, my daughter helped me to find a place to live, secured rental furniture and household items, and moved me into temporary housing. I am happy to report that I am okay."

Sometimes the strings to our past are burned because we need a new beginning. Few of us are willing to change our lives radically, in spite of all the intuitive signals we receive that something has to give. We will instead remain in the worst first-chakra situation—such as a brutal job or an unhappy marriage—rather than risk striking out on our own. Uprooting ourselves—a first-chakra challenge—and moving out of what is familiar can be overwhelming. But fate and destiny will intervene to redirect us. (Fate is how your life unfolds when you let fear determine your choices. A path of destiny reveals itself to you, however, when you confront your fear and make conscious choices.) Facing your circumstances without anger or despair and determining to make the best of things will empower your future.

One man told me that he had lost everything—his job and his marriage—in one day. Even so, he experienced one of the most conscious moments of his life during that critical day and realized that he had a choice; he could either become raging and bitter, consumed in his anger, or realize that only heaven can so perfectly sever one's connection to the past. He decided that the wise way to endure the depth of pain was to accept that there was a reason why his past had to be so immediately removed. He decided to move forward in faith and create a new life.

Linda T. lost her home in a tornado. "Within two days," wrote Linda, "the building where I lived with my children was condemned and evacuated for safety reasons. I had no extra money for such an event and no insurance. The moving company I called came to my rescue in record time, removed my furniture, put it in storage for half of the service charge, and allowed me to pay the balance when I could recover financially. It was a godsend."

When we realize we have received God-sent assistance, we tap into a reservoir of survival grace. The fact that people were inspired or moved through compassion to help Linda is like a message from the divine reminding us that we are not alone. Surviving traumas requires love and support from family, friends, neighborhood children, and even strangers. But it also requires that you find meaning and purpose in your experience and decide that you will endure.

Deborah P. writes of another trauma, "While my husband and I were overseas, our home was burglarized and many expensive items were stolen. Our neighbors looked after everything until our return on the next available flight. They even stayed until the glass repair person came, which was at 2 A.M. But the ultimate act of service was when these neighbors met us at the airport in order to support us when we had to face the aftermath of our home invasion." Such support reminds us that life and our personal connections are more valuable than possessions.

> *O God, protect our going out and our coming in. Let us share the hospitality of this home with all who visit us that those who enter here may know your love and peace.*
>
> —A PRAYER FOR BLESSING A HOME

Uprooting our lives and our family is unsettling and frightening. It's difficult to start over in a strange area, especially when we leave places that we dearly love. Welcoming a newcomer to the neighborhood—or to the office—can obviously help him or her adjust to life in a strange setting. When you accept outsiders into your tribe, you provide a symbolic baptism. The following letters briefly tell of the incredible difference an open heart makes.

Jennie M. wrote, "When I moved to New Zealand from Ireland, the other side of the world, people took time from their busy lives, families, and work to bring me to places and show me things that would make my settling here much easier. We didn't know anyone and knew very little about Auckland and New Zealand. I didn't ask [for help], but it was always volunteered and their friendship and sincere kindness meant that our transition from home was just like crossing the road to an old neighbor's house for a cup of tea."

Cora shared, "I came to Germany from Romania in 1987 from Communism under Ceauşescu. Two people invited my family to stay at their home and helped us with information we would need and gave us the warmth of a family. I now do the same because I feel that it is very important to have such support from a family so that someone can feel at home."

Welcoming Someone

May the Lord give you peace.
— THE GREETING OF ST. FRANCIS OF ASSISI

Coming home to friends and family is one of the sweetest experiences. At the same time, returning to the tribe or the home front can feel awkward because life on the outside can change us so much that fitting in again feels like trying to squeeze into old clothes. Your first chakra carries the roots of your childhood and simultaneously the roots you have planted as an adult. Sometimes the type of ground that suits you as an adult on your own journey is a lifetime away from the earth that you stood on as a child. Imagine that when someone returns home, that individual's first chakra goes into a type of overdrive, energetically trying to reconnect to circuits once so familiar, while trying to remain fully connected to his own home territory. Tuning in to this subtle dynamic is a way of accepting all the changes that have occurred in that person's life, and sends the message that no matter where you go or how your life changes for you, you will always be loved.

Cynthia D. wrote a lovely version of a homecoming in which her spirit as well as her body was welcomed back: "Upon my return home from India, my family welcomed me into our home. They had prepared it with beauty, something that is essential to my life. Fresh spring flowers were lovingly displayed around every room; the scents wrapped me in love; aromatherapy candles graced the tabletops. They had prepared fresh sushi. They had had the entire home cleaned and the dim lighting added to the gentleness of the moment. Wide-eyed and anticipatory, they watched my teary expression and hugged me for what felt like an eternity. Awed and overwhelmed, I accepted this sweetness and pleasure fully, and the experience shall live within me always."

Jenni A. describes the very real trauma to the spirit that occurs when we uproot ourselves and how stepping in to help someone through that transition is an invisible act of power that lasts a lifetime. "My father was in the military and our family moved overseas. We didn't have base housing yet and I was required to take a city bus a far distance to school. Normally I would be with my brother, but this day I missed the bus and wound up by myself. I was ten-years-old. I was a stranger in a strange land. I remember the fear of abandonment. I felt helpless. I didn't know what to do. I sat on the bus bench and sobbed. Then, suddenly, I felt the presence of someone I knew. My oldest sister had witnessed my dilemma and came to help me. She was in high school and was in a rush to catch her own bus. Instead, she took my hand and stood with me until the next bus to my school came along. During the hour ride, she held me close as my tears dried up. She softly sang to me. After making sure I got to school, my sister caught another bus to get to the high school.

She was late, but that didn't matter. She was more interested in soothing the tears and fears of her baby sister. I will never forget that. I still consider my oldest sister to be one of the dearest people I know."

Finally, there's coming home to Mom, a first-chakra need so primal that whether we have loving or tragic memories of our childhood, we never stop imagining a warm home for ourselves. Lisa S. wrote, "After I moved thousands of miles away, I came back to visit my hometown and was lovingly surprised to find out that my mom had bought all my favorite foods from my childhood days: Red Baron pizza, Little Debbie rolls, sparkling water, oranges. It was so thoughtful and giving of her. I could picture her rolling a cart through the aisles, a little slip of paper in hand, listing all my favorite things, dropping the items into the cart and taking them home—not for her, but for me . . . just to see me happy. I like to surprise people in just such a way. It's like proof that the world is a good place, full of people with the best intentions. Everyone needs to be reassured of that at some time."

Places of business can be among the most challenging tribes to break into. Just as intimidating as moving into a new town is taking a new job within a corporation or business because, in addition to having to learn the ropes of your new occupation, you also have to melt into a foreign social system. Anyone coming into a place for the first time is going to feel overwhelmed, nervous, and socially awkward and deeply appreciative of a warm welcome.

A woman named Ayn shared her initiation experience, writing, "I was a new employee and had been on the job for about three months when I walked in one morning and found a cute little glass tea keeper and bag caddy on the middle of my desk, along with a poem. The poem was about my being a valued member of the organization and the poem even included a reference to my being a tea drinker. I never knew who did this, but it was much appreciated because someone had gone to the trouble of getting to know a little about me personally and even more, took the time and effort to weave what they knew about me into a poem. It was one of those nice, warm 'You're a member of the team' moments and I will never forget it. I still have that little tea keeper."

A New Family

For most of the people I spoke with, offering shelter to someone, much less a family, is the one gift of the earth they would hesitate to provide. Jim summed up the fear most shared about sheltering someone when he said, "The risk in offering an individual or a family a place to stay is high in that they may not leave. Then they become your financial burden. I mean once people unpack their bags, it's very difficult to get them to move on. And what if they have no place to go? Are you going to kick them out into the street where you found them? So no, I would not be inclined to open the door of my home to someone who needed shelter. I would perhaps pay for a night for them at a hotel, but involving yourself with a homeless person is overwhelming because you might be the only one between the two of you who has any survival skills."

This very real fear makes the following stories all the more remarkable, beginning with the memory Rolando S. shared in his letter: "My stepfather and I never got along. When I was sixteen years old, I was told to leave home and never to return, visit, or call. I did not have any family that I could turn to, so I packed up my things and left, not knowing where to go. Interestingly enough, while I had no idea where to go and who to turn to, I was not afraid. Maybe it was the combination of being young and angry or perhaps it was that something deep down in me told me that this was the perfect way for my life to evolve. After sharing my situation with my best friend, Joey, he suggested that we talk to his parents. He was one of six siblings and one of his older brothers had just moved out, which meant there was a possible room for me in his home. I vividly recall standing in the family room of his house, explaining my situation to his parents. They offered to let me stay with them and my stay lasted over a year. Besides the immense act of kindness they provided by allowing me to stay with them, I also recall that during the holiday season, I did not want to be in the way or a burden. I was overwhelmed when I discovered that under the Christmas tree was a present with my name on it. These people were pivotal in my life. Had they not been there for me, my journey would have evolved much differently."

Rolando recognized that though his circumstance might not be easy, this situation was essential to the whole of his life's journey. Many, many people made similar statements in their letters, reporting that even in the midst of the worst crises, a sense of purpose would fill their being that temporarily eclipsed their fears, noting that this momentary encounter with grace was enough to sustain them through even the rigors of being without shelter.

I chose the following two letters (from well over one hundred similar letters) because these two women discovered that somehow even in the midst of the worst chaos, the universe still provides a map for our survival.

As Minerva C. discovered, "After almost eleven years of living in an abusive relationship, I was left 'all alone' with no place to go while also being totally responsible for my three sons and my mother. I asked my husband's brother and wife if we could stay with them for 'a while.' They never questioned me about the [possible] length of time of our stay. I will *never* forget their kindness. I am a firm believer that you do what you can for others less fortunate than you. I never regret helping others even if they don't appreciate it. I do what I can because I know in my heart it's the right thing."

Zoe wrote, "I had to look for a place to live because my now ex-husband pushed me, along with our daughters, out of the apartment. One evening, I visited a friend who happened to be with a person that I had only seen twice before. I told my friend that I had not been able to find a place to live and this other person said she had an apartment available. We immediately went to see it and the next day she gave me the key, even without references or a deposit, and all of us moved in. This woman was an angel. She offered me a place to live when I was at a breaking point in my life, without even knowing how desperate I was."

While gifts of shelter usually accompany dire situations, gifts of food can be spontaneous acts of love as well as lifesaving interventions. Providing a meal to someone creates a gratitude and love that last a lifetime.

The Gift of Food

Democracy and hunger cannot go together. A hungry stomach questions and censures the system's failure to meet what is a basic biological need of every human being. There can be no place for hunger and poverty in a modern world in which science and technology have created conditions for abundance.

—ATAL BIHARI VAJPAYEE, FORMER PRIME MINISTER OF INDIA

A man once asked the prophet what was the best thing in Islam and the latter replied, "It is to feed the hungry and to give the greeting of peace both to those one knows and to those one does not know."

—HADITH OF BUKHARI

At one of my workshops during a lunch break, one woman said to her companion, "I'm starving." A man who overheard them as they passed smiled at me and said, "I wonder what they would do if they were really starving. I know what I did. I picked through garbage cans. When I was a kid, it was the only way we could survive. You'll do anything if you're really hungry. When I moved to another country at age twenty-two, I wasn't able to find work, but I knew I could survive without food for a while and went days without eating. You never feel so helpless or humiliated as when you can't find a way to feed yourself."

I admired this man's spirit and his will to survive. The threat of starvation and hunger is very real to many people around the world. Feeding another person—whether it's a mother feeding her baby (as sanctified in innumerable portraits of the Blessed Virgin Mary nursing the infant Jesus) or taking meals to shut-ins and elderly people—has profound spiritual implications. Every world culture has deep associations of food with compassion, hospitality, and love for our fellow human beings. All spiritual leaders instruct us to feed those in need.

Sometimes healing through food comes at a critical time, as Ann S. noted in her letter: "I was going through a very emotionally trying time and as a result, lost quite a lot of weight. I had essentially stopped eating. One day a coworker, who I did not know very well, peeked over the divider and invited me out for a break. I don't know why, but something told me to go along, so I did. She was very kind and attentive and I just sort of followed along as she did errands. She never mentioned anything about my 'condition.' When we got to the drugstore, she picked up some multivitamins and different kinds of liquid energy drinks and when we returned to the office, she set the drinks and vitamins in front of me. She said she would like me to open the drink and just leave it on my desk, taking sips as I could throughout the day. She fetched a drink of water and opened the vitamins so I could take one.

"Each day she dropped by to see me and surreptitiously

checked to make sure I took a vitamin and was sipping my drink. She invited my toddler and me to her home and fed us both. She never pried into my personal life; she just told me that if I ever needed to talk, she was available. After a month, I had gained seven pounds and was much more functional. This wonderful person sensed it was time and started tapering off her daily visits and evening invitations. She had helped put me back on the road to health. She still doesn't know the full story of my traumatic experience and the subsequent spiritual journey that opened as a result. She was just someone who was there at the right time. We remain in touch to this day."

Bridget P. wrote, "I was having a very difficult day at work with lots to do and not enough time. A friend called and said, 'I know you're really busy and having a rough day so I was wondering if I could bring you dinner tonight?' He arrived with a 'comfort food' meal of all my favorite things—turkey, salad, good bread, and chocolate cake for dessert. I just had to sit down and eat. It meant the world to me that someone would care enough about my sustenance to offer something that I needed and would have been too proud or busy to ask for."

Pat J. offers the perspective of the provider, writing, "I am inclined to cook a meal for people if I know they are having a hard time or feeling stressed. I've done that many times for older neighbors, friends with small children, and even my son's teacher when I know it's a hectic time of the school year. I love to cook and I know people appreciate a home-cooked meal. It's nourishment for the body and soul and it lets people know you care. I try to make it special with the presentation or little touches, like flavored tea bags and cookies for dessert. I do it with love and I want that love to come through the meal."

The care and attention that it takes to prepare a meal for someone can be a genuine act of healing as well as an act of love, as Carol W. discovered: "One of the most meaningful things anyone ever did for me happened the day my mother died. Our wonderful neighbor across the street, to whom we were not especially close, brought an entire meal for nine of us over to our house. I can still see the roast, smell the potatoes, and recall the wonderful sense of being cared for as a result of that act of service. It was a complete surprise and I will always be grateful to them."

Love and personal attention are deeply healing. Add food to that and you have a sacred meal that nurtures the spirit while feeding the body. I love Alice W.'s story because she so perfectly captures the alchemy of a sacred meal: "A few years ago, I had an accident that kept me pretty immobile for a couple of months. I was a graduate student at the time as well as a single mom. My daughter was seven years old and in desperate need of the type of attention that I could not provide, much less the sort of nutrition that comes from conscious food preparation. At first, my friends were eager and willing to do whatever they could for me, but after five or six weeks of being dependent upon the good will of others, the well dries up. I did my best, but I was in a great deal of pain and exhausted from worry and the stress of being housebound and in need of physical therapy. One night, I just started to cry and my crying led me to praying. In my prayers, I informed heaven that I was at a breaking point and that while I could handle this situation, what I could not deal with was that my young daughter had to cope with so much, including preparing her own meals, which had been reduced to sandwiches and cookies. The next day, a friend of mine came over with an entire carton full of homemade meals frozen in about two dozen Tupperware containers. And not only that, she stayed to prepare a feast for my daughter and me. And as if that wasn't enough of an answer to my prayer, she pulls out a sweet prayer book that she kept at her bedside and read aloud three prayers asking for healing. I was never so touched in my life. And I have never once since that time felt alone in this Universe."

W.'s story illustrates that the preparation of a meal becomes an act of spiritual alchemy—an invisible act of power—that ushers in genuine healing energies, kind of like gourmet prayers. "In December 1990, I was a stay-at-home mom with three young children coping with an out-of-work husband who checked himself into a mental hospital. I was without income coming into the Christmas season. Many miracles happened that month. The pastor gave me money for rent and utility bills and friends gave us a Christmas tree and gifts. But for some reason, the most meaningful gift that I recall was when people from my church began pulling up each evening with a meal for us. My knee-jerk reaction was, 'No, not me! I give to other people. I'm not supposed to be on the receiving end!' And then I realized what a blessing it was to have the decision of what to serve my children for dinner made for me. I was relieved of a major responsibility and I learned the blessing of being a 'cheerful receiver.' Now I know the significance of a meal, delivered to the family, in love and caring. This is now the act of service I give to others."

Many people sent letters that said their most significant healing experience came through the kitchen. We can invoke a profound spiritual power when we nourish and nurture others, with the intention to comfort and heal. We can reach out to people through food because food is one gift of the heart that so easily can embrace the intention of the heart. Recently I had a conversation with a friend of mine who is a pastry chef. Her heart philosophy, or the secret of her success, is, in her own words, "the fact that I am absolutely aware that I am feeding my clients. I am preparing special treats that they eat on special occasions. I want the desserts I make to be as much a part of their memories of an anniversary party or a birthday as the gifts they receive that day from friends."

First-Chakra Health and Spirituality

Serve people and feed people.

—NEEM KAROLI BABA

Assume from now on that you are an intuitive being within a physical body. In fact, you are always doing intuitive readings. Once you shift from observing to sensing a person's crisis, the decision whether to do something becomes a spiritual matter, not a social one.

First-chakra actions bring the grace that makes us feel good about our life again. Our basic survival no longer seems impossible. The first principle of a first-chakra theology would be that we are meant to care about each other and the well-being of the entire human family because our physical survival and spiritual survival depend on one another. We are drawn to help each other, to be there for one another, because we are made of the same spiritual substance.

Examining the Heart of Your First Chakra

Please take time to consider the following questions to explore how compassion and purpose manifest in your life. It is vitally important to your personal growth to become aware of your motivations for giving. The ideal as taught by the spiritual masters is to become comfortable—empowered—enough to give and serve unconditionally. Nonetheless, the generosity of your first chakra typically begins with visible acts of service that minister to the basic needs of survival. We begin our path of service by learning to care for our family, friends, and community. The kindness and compassion we carry within us are more powerful than all the material goods we can provide.

With this in mind, please ask yourself:

1. Do you think in terms of helping your own kind as opposed to just helping others?
2. Do you see society as a fundamentally generous body of power or do you see the world as a place where only the fittest survive?
3. Do you feel an obligation to give back to society because of your own accomplishments?
4. Do you see yourself as essentially on your own or do you actively nurture your tribal, social, and community support systems?
5. Can you be counted on? Or do you count yourself out? Do other people think of you as generous and helpful or unapproachable?
6. Have you ever put limits on how much you are willing to help someone? What are those limits based on? Limits are often based on wisdom and experience, so please do not assume that limits are a negative. But note if the limits you set come from a fear of not having enough or adherence to other myths about power.
7. Have you ever needed the support of others? In what way? Did you receive the assistance you needed? Was it more or less than you had hoped for?

I've closed this chapter with the beautiful Serenity Prayer because it helps us address the challenges in our lives that are meant to make us grow. A part of that growth includes discovering that we really do need other people, that we are all one.

A FIRST-CHAKRA PRAYER

THE SERENITY PRAYER
God grant me the serenity
to accept the things I cannot change;
courage to change the things I can;
and wisdom to know the difference.
Living one day at a time;
Enjoying one moment at a time;
Accepting hardships as the pathway to peace.
Taking, as He did, this sinful world
as it is, not as I would have it;
Trusting that He will make all things right
if I surrender to His Will;
That I may be reasonably happy in this life
and supremely happy with Him.
Forever in the next.
    Amen.

—REINHOLD NIEBUHR

Gifts of Financial and Creative Support

*God is present in every act of service. All life turns on this law. . . .
Whoever violates it, indulging his sense for his own pleasure and
ignoring the needs of others, has wasted his life.*
— The Bhagavad Gita

Two friends are chatting together one day and in the course of their conversation, one man asks the other, "If you had two houses, would you give me one?"

"Of course I would," he replied.

His friend continued, "And if you had two boats, would you give me one?"

Again his friend said, "Well, of course I would. We are good friends and what are good friends for?"

They both paused for a moment, basking in the warm feelings they had for each other. Then, the man asked his friend a third question, "And if you had two chickens, would you give me one of them?"

"No," replied his friend.

Astonished by this change in his friend's generosity, the man inquired, "But why not? You would give me one of your houses and one of your boats, but not a chicken? I don't understand."

"Simple," replied the man. "I *have* two chickens."

Generosity can be a challenge if we are worried about having enough ourselves. Insecurities about our daily survival are rooted in the lower chakras. You can even see this reflected in your body language. Whenever you feel uncomfortable or insecure, you automatically cover or protect the physical areas of your second and third chakras. For instance, you cross your hands over the area below your waist (second chakra), or fold your arms over your solar plexus or stomach (third chakra). Women frequently put their purses on their laps as a shield between external energy and their second and third energy centers. And stress on your second chakra—especially financial stress—primarily affects your lower back.

Yet financial stress does not necessarily mean financial hardship. Often, quite the opposite is true. I have met many people, for instance, whose stress comes from feeling acutely the pain of the people they help. One woman who heads a foundation dedicated to helping families survive natural disasters said to me, "It is impossible to be impersonal about the crises of the people who come to us. You want to take them in your arms and promise them everything will be all right again. I am very grateful that I can be of some help to them, but I have to tell you that it is a heavy burden when I have to tell some that funds have run out. Invariably, though, when that happens, the community does come forward to help." The pressure on this woman as manager of a charity frequently results in lower back pain. She admitted that she sometimes felt guilty for being better off than the people to whom she was providing physical aid, and she often felt uncomfortable having to tell someone there was no money for him when she personally had a full wallet. It's not easy to work this close to the fire of social need, but getting burned won't help you or the people you're serving. This kind of pain is not inevitable. It is the consequence of wanting life to be what it can never be, which is perfect.

The Consciousness of Your Second Chakra

The second chakra's key word is *relationship*. At this level, your energy shifts from how you relate to your environment to how you relate to individuals—one on one—*within* your environment. The second chakra is the sensor on which you rely primarily to evaluate others' energy fields.

Second-chakra power is involved in every exchange you make—including monetary exchanges. It houses the energy of making "covenants," and the Christian sacrament of Communion, which represents our one-on-one relationship with God, is a spiritual symbol for this energy. Every relationship in our life has a sacred component that we are meant to honor. "Honor one another" is this energy's motto. And every time we acknowledge the divinity in another person we're dealing with, whether he or she is a friend, family member, lover, coworker, teacher, student, neighbor, adversary, or stranger, our second level of power is at work.

Whereas the first chakra symbolizes our need for the physical safety of the group, the second chakra moves us into the world of money, sexuality, creativity, procreativity, partnership, and empowerment of the other. In the natural course of growing up, we are taught to nourish, clothe, and shelter ourselves, to be a part of a family and tribe. In a healthy family, we are also taught to recognize the importance of others in our lives, to take a mate, to reach out from our protected self and engage with others to create relationships and to forge our own life. This is the organic way in which we learn that we all are one and even if those specific words are not taught to us, we develop an inner sense of their spiritual truth.

We may also learn that empowering another person—whether through love, creative or financial support, or compassion and kindness—is ultimately also an act of self-empowerment. No one is born comfortable in this truth, however, because second-chakra energy also contains our inborn sense of competition. It adheres to the fears that there is not enough to go around and empowering you will cost me. A wise nun and professor of mine once told me, "Never let the fear of what another person can do or what he or she can become determine the essential goodness of your soul. If you have a giving soul, then give. If you don't, then learn."

Nothing about being human is as simple as "Just say yes." We are not compassionate just because we are meant to be that way. We learn to expand our hearts to include others because of what we have been taught, because of our own experiences, and because of how we see our relationship to God. How and why we care for others is a complex part of our spiritual evolution, even though we might attribute our nature to being "just the way I am."

There is no such thing as a simple act of compassion or an inconsequential act of service. Everything we do for another person has infinite consequences. Every action gives rise to a ripple effect, just as a pebble that is tossed into a pond sends out wave after wave, widening and covering more and more space. Everything we do and say matters. Period. This is why Buddhists and Hindus, indeed all the great spiritual traditions, teach the importance of mindfulness in speech and attention to behavior, because of the limitless, unforeseen effects of our every action and word. Even our thoughts have a force and power about which we have to be careful.

Because the way of the spirit is inherently one of service, people are sent to us who are meant to help us see our path. Others will always be sent our way when needed so that we learn the truth that "What goes around comes around."

Anne D. wrote, "As a young man, my husband went through a time of being without a clear direction. He was without a job and without a place to stay, feeling pretty hopeless about his life in general. Then he received a call from an old friend he hadn't seen or heard from in at least five years, who told him that he was living an hour away, working on starting a ski hill. He said, 'I remembered how much you love this area and I wanted to let you know that there may very well be a job for you here, if you can show up tomorrow morning.'

"Since we didn't have a car, my husband hitchhiked to the area and was hired. As a result of that one call, my husband spent the next twenty-seven years learning how to make and groom snow. He went from having no money, no job, no car, and no place to live to becoming a highly valued member of a ski hill team where he's known for his 'gift for getting' snow so perfectly that he can create it and make it perform in ways that few people can. One phone call from out of the blue from an old friend made all the difference to my husband who, as a result, truly found himself and discovered his gift."

Second-chakra generosity typically means helping people financially or creatively, or providing means of healing. People who have received such help feel enormous gratitude, and people who have provided this type of assistance to others also feel grateful for the opportunity to serve. In many of the letters I received, people revealed that they felt compelled to share their good fortune. Many were also inspired to give back to others.

The Gift of Financial Intervention

Too many have dispensed with generosity in order to practice charity.

— ALBERT CAMUS

Many people reach their breaking point, or symbolically, their opportunity for transformation, just as their physical ability to move stops or their "car" breaks down. In dream and symbolic interpretation, cars represent traveling down the road of one's own life journey. Like St. Paul, who had a profound turning point on the road to Damascus, where he could not move for several days after the Lord spoke to him, many people report that their breakdown or inability to move physically enabled them to see the opportunities for change that they otherwise may have missed. In ancient mythology, Hermes was the god who often appeared to travelers. He was a trickster god, a magician figure, and carried a flaming wand entwined by two snakes or caduceus (the symbol of healing). Often he would appear to travelers in the guise of a coincidental meeting that turned out to be somehow significant as a catalyst on the journey—the god of synchronicity! Hermes was the god of the crossroads, whose blessing was invoked by travelers, wanderers, and the homeless. But Hermes would also appear to ancient people as a sudden hunch, or in the discovery that one knows more than one thought.

In the light of the myth and legend surrounding roads and journeys and divine interventions, it seems appropriate to group some contemporary stories of modern angels.

Siobhan wrote, "A few years ago, I had put a deposit down on an apartment and the next day, with funds already tight, I was laid off from my job. I was terrified and while driving to the post office, I thought that God is testing my faith. I decided to put my trust in God's hands. Then I hit the curb and punctured the two new tires I had put on my old car. I got out of my car, put my head on the bonnet, and sobbed. Then I heard a man ask me what was wrong. I looked up at a Latino man standing in the driveway of a mechanics shop, noticing that I had managed to blow out my tires right in front of a repair shop. It turned out that this man was the owner. I wailed about losing my job, having no money and now no wheels on my car. He talked me through the situation, gently pointing out that I had made some poor choices regarding the job that landed me in this situation in the first place. Then he told one of his workers to put some used tires on my car. He gave them to me as a gift, which not only brought me home, but they lasted six months. The next day, as I was leaving my old job, I happened to run into a man I knew who owned a law firm. I asked him for a job right on the spot, which I eventually obtained. I am incredibly grateful to the God that is within and 'without.' "

In another story in which money and car problems converged, Karen P. wrote, "Many years ago I was going through a very difficult divorce from a man with a cocaine addiction, who had spent all our money. As a result, we lost our home. Then the car I was driving was hit by a drunk driver and irreparably damaged and I didn't have car insurance. Ironically, at the time I was the director of a domestic violence legal aid project and needed transportation for work. A judge I knew suggested that I go to a particular used-car lot to get another car; he thought the people working there might help me. There I did find a used car for four thousand dollars. The bank was willing to finance a loan for me, but they were not allowed by law to provide the down payment I required. I had tears rolling down my face at the car dealership, not knowing what to do, and then the car dealer, whom I had never met before in my life, told me that he admired what I did to help others. He personally loaned me the down payment. He told me that he knew my life would turn around so until I could get my kids settled, get a divorce, and get back on my feet, he would take care of the down payment. I have never forgotten this man and his incredible act of kindness. And things did turn around and my life is blessed today."

Rose C. remembered: "I had a hairstyling client who was very dear to me. She was highly intelligent, determined, very giving, and a seeker of things out of the norm. She believed in my psychic abilities and encouraged me not to let my light sit under a bushel. She often lifted me up in her own way. When she died, much to my surprise I found she had left a nice sum of money to me. I was floored. She had commented to me about dreams she wanted to help along, but I was at a loss as to what she had perceived as my dream. I remembered she asked why I was doing hair instead of using my abilities to help people. Ultimately, I used the money to help my family and pay off some debt, to give my girls some money for school, and help a friend who was out of work. It was a gift that became several gifts. I now do readings for people at no charge or on a donation-only basis to continue the giving, for I knew she wanted me to use my gifts. She made me seek what I wanted if I were not hindered by finances. I sincerely hope I honored her spirit of giving in what I did with her gift to me."

Anticipate charity by preventing poverty; assist the reduced fellow man, either by a considerable gift or a sum of money or by teaching

him a trade or by putting him in the way of business so that he may
earn an honest livelihood and not be forced to the dreadful alternative
of holding out his hand for charity. This is the highest step and
summit of charity's golden ladder.

—MAIMONIDES

Doubtless you are capable of spotting the wisdom hidden in the crises of those around you, especially those most dear to you. We're great at that. But the journey to spiritual maturity requires that you review the incidents or crises in your life to find the wisdom or purpose they contain. It is present in every experience. Has guidance come into your life when you were vulnerable? Did you follow it? Would you have listened to that guidance if you hadn't been in a crisis? Or would you have had the courage to make changes—to approach someone for a job, for example— had the universe not set the stage for you to step out and take action? Invisible power is always in motion. Even when you don't know how help will ever reach you in time, somehow the heavens will move the earth on your behalf . . . although rarely in the way you expect. But notice also that when your heart is moved by compassion to help others, you often become a source of guidance or wisdom for them. You are especially effective when you are free of any personal motives. In the preceding two stories, both women benefited from the guidance of objective people who could see clearly for them.

Janice P. shared her experience with an intuitive intervention: "Several years ago, when my husband was out of work and the bills were coming in from everywhere, I received a check in the mail from my brother. I thought it was to help with the bills or buy groceries, but his specific instructions were that I not pay one bill or buy any food. He knew that the needle on our stereo was broken and that we couldn't even afford to replace that as other things were more important. He requested that we replace the stereo needle, buy a bottle of wine and a couple of steaks, and have a relaxing romantic evening on him. He knew how stressful a time it was for us and he wanted to give us a break from our situation. That night we had our wine and steaks and listened to our favorite music and escaped from everything that was bringing us down. It meant so much to me that he knew, more than I did, how badly we needed that night."

> *The world's affairs and the floating clouds—*
>   *why question them?*
> *You had best take life easily—and have a good dinner.*
> — "GIVING P'EI TI A DRINK" IN
>   *THE POEMS OF WANG WEI* (699–761)

Another story of a similar intervention is told by Samantha J.: "When my husband and I moved to San Diego, we had about two cents to rub together. We simply loaded up our car and moved, not knowing anyone in San Diego. We rented an apartment and found jobs, but our money was tight. Out of the blue, my brother sent us a check for twenty-five dollars, which was a lot of money at the time. We were living paycheck to paycheck and right before Bill's check arrived, we were wondering how we were going to buy food for that week. I will never forget how relieved and grateful we were when his check arrived. As a result of that, I am inclined to give money anonymously. I am by no means wealthy, but when I hear about someone struggling financially, I will send them a hundred-dollar bill in one of those cards that says, 'Hang in there.' I do not sign it and I usually mail it from somewhere outside my zip code. It gives me great pleasure to do this and the inspiration for it came from my brother, Bill."

*   *   *

Riches and power are but gifts of blind fate, whereas goodness is the result of one's own merit.

—Héloïse of Abelard

Many letters I received expressed surprise at the other people's honesty in returning money or lost belongings. In fact, I heard a story on the news recently in which a small-town hardware store received a drill in the mail that the sender had stolen fifty years ago. He now felt compelled to return it, saying that he did so because, "I know angels watch what we do" and included a hundred-dollar bill in payment. Acts of honesty and integrity regarding property are second-chakra responsibilities. People are as amazed by acts of honesty as they are by acts of kindness. Honesty as a personal practice—truthfulness of action, word, and thought—should rightly be considered an invisible act of power.

I chose the following letter because the author was the recipient of several coordinated invisible acts of power. Mary Lynn A. wrote, "When I was pregnant with our first child, my husband was still in school and I was working as a massage therapist. We were broke. Our regular mail came to our home address but we had a post office box for correspondence about workshops we taught. We checked that box at least two to three times a week. One Saturday morning, we found a 'final' notice to check with a postal worker. Neither of us remembered receiving a first or second notice. We turned in the notice and the postmaster told us that it was a good thing that we came for this letter because it was about to be sent to the dead-letter center. The envelope was filled with ten one-hundred-dollar bills and nothing else. The envelope was hand addressed with an illegible postmark and no return address, and it was ripped and mangled. Not only had someone anonymously sent that money, but one or more postal workers who handled that damaged envelope had to have known there was money in it, but they left it there and made sure it got to us. To this day we have no idea where that money came from, but that money was such a remarkable gift. It helped us through a couple of difficult months but more important, it helped reaffirm our belief in the abundance of the universe. So far we haven't been able to give a thousand dollars at a time, but we do give smaller anonymous gifts of financial support because I know how it felt to be on the receiving end. It makes being on the giving end all the more special."

The Gift of Creative Support

The man of perfect virtue, wishing to be established himself, seeks also to establish others; wishing to be enlarged himself, he seeks also to enlarge others.

— CONFUCIUS

Every single person is born with something to create—that creation might be a child or a business or a garden or a circle of friends or a peace accord. Whatever it is will be personally beneficial as well as beneficial for others. Blocked creative expression is as detrimental to your well-being as a drug addiction. A raging internal conflict between acting on creative impulses or settling for the status quo can eventually promote physical illness. This internal strife locks into the second chakra first and foremost because this is the vortex where you act on your convictions. You need to manifest your ideas and to make a difference in your world, whether your influence is enormous or small. The size of your action or gift is not the issue; the *act* of creation is.

Creativity is also essential to your spiritual health. Supporting someone else's creative ideas or efforts is the same thing as supporting his or her spiritual journey in this lifetime. No one can manifest his or her creative gifts alone; we need each other. Every artist needs someone to look at or listen to or appreciate his creation. Every child needs multiple caretakers who appreciate her unique attributes. We are sent into the lives of people who need creative support just as people are sent into our lives. Sometimes all that we need to do is provide invisible psychological support. "You can do it" or "Hang in there" can be a source of renewed faith. Any support you give to another person's creative dreams is an act of spiritual ignition.

What the gods ask of us, what they watch for in our actions, words, and thoughts, is whether we are generous enough to help a fellow traveler on this planet. Imagine that a celestial spotlight shines on you when an opportunity arises for you to be a positive force in someone's life; the actual situation tests the quality of your faith and the depth of your generosity. Perhaps it is simply the opportunity to congratulate someone for an academic or professional accomplishment. Perhaps it's the birth of a new baby or a child's first sports trophy. These all test the generosity of your spirit. It's much easier to buy a meal for a homeless person you don't know than to forgive someone you do know for having more than you. If you find it difficult to celebrate another's accomplishments, remember that your reaction is being watched from above.

Get on with your own creative life. Ideas are free. They don't cost you a thing. You can live in the world of thought all the days of your life and never go broke. You will also die unfulfilled, because an idea that never incarnates, that never becomes physical and grounded in this world, will eventually feel like the most painful burden you ever had to carry—one that you can never put down. People who have had near-death experiences report that there is indeed a life review that happens upon our death, and that a part of that life review is to make note of what could have been in our lives had we chosen otherwise. Falling into that category are all the creative opportunities the universe provided for us that we let fall by the wayside because our fears carried more authority within us than our faith. Trust in the life support system that is inherent in your creative spirit. You will draw to yourself all that you need as you need it, but you must first be willing to risk it all. That's why I love the following stories of people who received gifts of creative support from others just when they needed it most.

Shelagh C. shares her exquisite talent for providing creative support to others: "I think passing on information can be a wonderful act of service. In my life, people who have recommended specific books that turned out to be tremendously helpful to me at that particular stage of my journey have done me a great service. Learning basic life skills relies very much on getting the information you need at the right time and if, as in my case, you grew up being discouraged from asking questions, it can set you up for disastrous decision-making skills that can take years to repair. It's a theme in my life, and therefore no accident, that I'm working in the reference department of a public library. It's very satisfying to get people the information they need at the time they need it. And sometimes I get to act on my intuition and push something under the nose of someone who isn't yet aware of their need, but inevitably they thank me for it later."

Along those same lines, Suzy C. wrote, "I recently graduated from massage therapy school and opened my own part-time practice. My teacher surprised me with what I consider a very generous act of service which meant the world to me. One evening as I was busy cleaning and painting my newly rented office space, she stopped by to see me. She said she had been inspired to book an appointment for every month over the next year. She did so, saying that when she had first started out as a massage therapist, a client had done the same thing for her, telling her that now she could tell people that she was booked up to a year in advance. Because of that, her confidence and self-esteem as a massage therapist got a significant boost—as did mine. Many times I have marveled over her generosity of spirit and have been motivated to 'put my money where my mouth is' by supporting and affirming students from our local college who did a production of *The Vagina Monologues*. I loved the performance—the play has an incredible message for women and men—and felt so extremely proud of each young woman. I wanted to do something to honor them. So I sent a gift certificate for one free massage to each of the thirty-four students in the production. It was my way of saying, 'What you did is important.' "

The content of these letters validates again and again the intimate connection we share with each other and with the universe. They are living proof of the power and wisdom contained in the world's spiritual teachings.

Jennifer H. wrote briefly of a significant encounter: "I was entering a local mall. At the doorway stood a rather disheveled man who was ringing a bell for the Salvation Army. I spoke to him and blessed him as I put some money into his kettle. Upon entering the store, a woman stopped me and said, 'I saw you and how you spoke to that man outside. It is a mark of good human character when you do something for those who can do nothing for you in return. Thank you for being to kind to that sad-looking person.' For some reason, her kind words have stayed with me to this day, many years later. In my way of thinking, she performed a wonderful act of service for me by acknowledging my humanity."

And Kay S. wrote of an act of service that raised her self-esteem and helped her to step back into the world. "I think an act of service comes in different packages, such as a cherished memory as a result of someone thinking of you or a special gift that meant the world to you. In an act of service for me, a friend brought me a bathing suit bottom wrap. I have gained some fifty pounds plus since I stopped smoking a year and a half ago. I love the ocean and my friend knew how much I missed it this year because I felt too fat to go to the beach. It was such a gift that she had me on her mind and brought this to me. She told me, 'Now you can go to the ocean. You can slide into the water and no one will even notice you.' It really touched my heart."

Charity sees the need, not the cause.

— GERMAN PROVERB

When you offer creative support with no expectations for yourself, you are giving support. Yet many of these letters prove that what we do for others is always, in some way, given back to us, as Deborah G. discovered: "I helped a friend create a brochure for her public relations business. She is not a writer or competent with computer programs and I happen to be good at both. I offered to help because I enjoy putting together information. The final product was delivered yesterday and without telling me, she forwarded a copy of the brochure to the head of a national woman's organization that she belongs to, suggesting that they consider using me to create brochures for them. I was speechless when she sent me an e-mail telling me what she had done."

The no-strings-attached gift is an invisible act of power precisely because it carries no expectations or obligations. It seems to have particular potency for enhancing creative energies of people, as the following individuals discovered.

Kara B. wrote, "A coworker and his wife gifted me with several terms worth of tuition to continue my education. I would have had to drop out otherwise. There were no strings attached except to one day help someone in the same way. I always try to help others I meet, even if it is just with a smile or a kind word. I am motivated by a driving need to make my existence on this planet mean something. I don't want to be rich and famous, but I want to make a difference."

And Teren E. wrote, "When I was a young, struggling dancer and couldn't find the money to take dance classes, a world-renowned teacher/choreographer simply told me to come to class anyway. When I could pay, great, and when I couldn't, it didn't matter. His generosity was effortless, simple, and completely unconditional. He taught me the true meaning of giving. Perhaps because of this early experience, I have come to regard true acts of service as those that are unheralded and given without waiting for someone to ask. I like to inspire confidence in friends and clients by recognizing their strengths and talents, and as a teacher myself, I am able to offer dedicated students classes for free when they have financial troubles. It seems the least I can do to return the favor to the universe." Teren's last phrase caught my attention: "Returning the favor to the universe" is a wonderful way to look upon the good we do for others. It also recognizes how aware the universe is of the details of our lives.

The Gift of Healing

An ancient traditional story tells of Shiva, the Hindu god of many forms, who often traveled in the guise of a beggar or a stranger in trouble. One day he arrived bruised and battered at the house of a sage. The sage's wife took him in and tended his wounds, treating him as a mother would her own child. She bathed him, fed him, and put him to bed. Shiva was so pleased by her compassion and care that he revealed his identity and rewarded her.

Health crises are critical times for helping. The kind of healing assistance you can offer often reflects your own vulnerabilities or your own experiences. Responding to someone's need for financial support during an illness is a form of second-chakra healing support. (Being available to listen, comfort, and offer counseling is a sixth-chakra act of power, about which we'll talk in chapter 6. Putting your heart into weeks or months of nursing someone is a fourth-chakra act of power.) We respond from our strength; not everyone is a good listener and not everyone is a good organizer. Many people know what they are good at, such as remaining calm in a crisis and being able to take charge when a family has collapsed in grief, classic first- and second-chakra strengths. Other people are best one on one, which is more of a third-chakra talent. Not everyone has the spiritual stamina to do that. While we are all different, each of us has at least one strong suit on which to draw to help others heal.

I have had several conversations over the years with people who have struggled to forgive members of their family or friends for not being there when they needed them most in healing crises. As I read through the letters I received, I realized that given the differences in our strengths and vulnerabilities, not everyone knows how to help appropriately. One man who wrote is still dealing with his wife's anger at what she felt was his unresponsiveness to her during her recovery from a car accident that left her bedridden for almost five months. Yet, he said, he offered to have the house remodeled so that she could move around more easily; he offered to put in an elaborate home entertainment unit so that she could fill the hours of her day watching movies; and he offered to set up a computer system by her bed.

He would have rearranged or bought her anything in order to help her through her recovery. In this, he was completely second-chakra generous, but what she felt she needed was fourth-chakra support—emotional nurturing, which for her meant an increase in attention and conversation. Neither understood the other's needs, because the crisis had created a new, unfamiliar complex of needs. Yet this man was as devoted and generous as he could be.

No one I know speaks chakras fluently enough to describe himself according to his chakra strengths and limitations, but we all order our lives unconsciously around the strengths and vulnerabilities of our energy system. Your intuition responds when others' needs match your strengths and vice versa. You can assume that if someone offers you assistance, somehow she has picked up signals that you are transmitting. You are not obligated to step forward to help or to accept assistance that is offered to you. But as you become conscious of the power in every single interaction, you develop a psychic common sense. Use it to guide you to accept assistance from people on your wavelength and to offer it.

The following stories are wonderful examples of how people on the same wavelength are brought together by the universe, as if it were consciously matching pairs of givers and receivers. Imagine the many cosmic details that had to come together in order to put these people at the same place at the right time. Coincidences and synchronicity require a great deal of cosmic organization. Keep this in mind next time you're wondering why it takes so much time to get answers to your prayers. Answers are acts of spiritual choreography—cosmic artwork at its best. And good art takes time.

Dorothy R. wrote, "One of my dearest friends has had cancer for seven years and recently she was near death. She wanted to go to Brazil to see a healer. Her plan was to go alone but I wanted to go with her as it was a long trip, but money was an issue for me. I prayed for her to have a safe trip and decided that if it were meant for me to go with her, somehow it would happen. One week later, the owner of the company where I work said he had heard that my friend wanted to go to Brazil and expressed his concern that she was going alone. I shared with him that the cost of the trip was prohibitive for me. The next day he placed an envelope inside my desk with two thousand dollars in cash. A week after we returned from Brazil, the doctor said my friend would not live. However, she is now feeling better and the miracle of Brazil is in progress."

The next two stories are particularly moving because they illustrate the power one person or one family has to inspire the goodness and generosity in a community of people without asking for help. Victoria B. wrote, "In 1997, I was working at the Tennessee Arts Commission as the gallery director. While helping to set up an exhibit, I lifted a crate of rocks and crushed a part of my spinal column. I lost all feelings in both arms, hands, and upper back. As a result, I became an 'injured worker on worker's compensation' for the state of Tennessee. My doctor performed three surgeries and kept me out of work. Needless to say, the state was not happy and so they stopped my worker's comp payments. I used up my savings and was ready to lose my house when a friend came over with a bowl of soup. She could feel my panic. She quickly organized a committee of friends who set up a daily schedule so that someone was with me in the morning and in the evening. They fed, bathed, and read to me in addition to purchasing groceries for over six months. It was during these six months that they decided to have a "Friends of Victoria" art fund-raiser. They contacted two hundred-plus artists that I have worked with in the gallery and asked each artist to donate a piece of art to sell. They secured a gallery, installed the show, and invited people to purchase the art in order to save my home. This fund-raiser was attended by well over five hundred people with whom I had worked throughout my career. I have never felt so much love in my life. The committee of friends saved my spirit and my home by raising over twenty thousand dollars in one night. Today I am able to hold a job and my doctors call me their 'miracle patient.' My purpose in life now is to help as many artists and people as I can."

And Gabrielle J. wrote, "Years ago, a woman who worked at my husband's office found out that we were going to seek an expensive educational treatment for our autistic son. She knew my husband didn't make a great deal of money, so she organized a fund-raising pool party, garage sale, and direct-deposit donation fund for us, all without consulting us. At first I was embarrassed, but then I realized what a gift this was. So many people came up to us and thanked us because it was so important for them to be able to help out. I remember going into the bathroom at the garage sale and crying after someone voiced their gratitude to me. This woman's generosity not only helped us financially, but it also helps us feel loved and support and it ended up giving others the power to make a difference, too."

Invisible acts of power are always unfolding in our lives, even without our having to ask. Our spirits and energy fields reach out for help even when our personalities find it uncomfortable to ask. I believe the stories people sent me validate the popular conception that when we release our needs and prayers to the universe *without strings attached*, the heavens take care of coordinating the outcome. This might appear to be a cosmic placebo, but it's not. Our universe has an impersonal design and an invisible divine energy, but it intimately connects all the souls within it.

Examining the Heart of
Your Second Chakra

The following asks you to examine your own needs and personal faith—your personal theology. These are exercises in self-discovery. The second chakra is your perceptual center for relationships and for how you perceive matters of survival in terms of finances, personal control, earthly power, and competition. You intuitively sense everything and everyone's energy before your conscious mind does. You are always doing intuitive readings, even when you tell yourself that your decisions are based on facts.

Now, consider these questions:

1. Upon meeting someone new, what is the first type of feedback you seek in order to establish familiarity: finances? Occupation or lack of one? Material goods or power? A sense of whether he or she feels like a good person?

2. Do you tend to judge someone harshly at first and then soften your opinion once you come to know him or her or do you withhold an opinion until you know that person better?

3. Do you negatively and quickly judge another person by his or her circumstances?

4. Do you jump to conclusions about how people could solve their problems?

5. Are you inclined to offer help without asking if someone needs it or not?

6. How do you decide whether to help someone?

7. Have you ever turned down a request for help? If
   so, why?
8. Are you uncomfortable around people who need help?

A SECOND-CHAKRA PRAYER

Each of us at some point needs to ask for help from heaven or other people. No doubt you've already been in that situation once or twice. If you are in what I would call a second-chakra crisis—financial, employment, or relationship—then take a moment now to release a prayer into the heavens, requesting divine intervention:

"God, please help me."

Now, let it go. Hold in your mind and in your heart your problem or fears and pray, "I release my fears into your guiding wisdom."

Look upon everything from the end of this prayer onward as having a part to play in the answer to your prayer . . . even if you end up hitting a curb driving to work and get two flat tires. Your prayer is heard instantly and just as instantly a response begins to make its way to you. I wish I could reach through the pages of this book and take hold of your hand to assure you of that.

Remember the words of the Third Psalm:

You, O LORD, are a shield for me,
My glory and the One who lifts up my head.
I cried to the LORD with my voice,
And He heard me from His holy hill. Selah

I lay down and slept;
I awoke, for the LORD sustained me.
I will not be afraid of ten thousands of people
Who have set themselves against me all around.

CHAPTER 3

Gifts of Self-Esteem

*Do not seek to benefit only yourself, but think of other people also.
If you yourself have an abundance, do not say, "The others do not
concern me, I need not bother about them!" If you were lucky in
hunting, let others share it. Moreover, show them the favorable
spots where there are many sea lions which can be easily slain.
If you want to amass everything for yourself, other people will stay
away from you and no one will want to be with you. If you should
one day fall ill, no one will visit you because, for your part, you did
not formerly concern yourself about others. Grant other people
something also. The Yamana do not like a person who acts selfishly.*
— YAMANA ESKIMO INITIATION

Some years ago, I was teaching a workshop on developing intuition and trying to help my students focus better on hearing their inner voice. I tried techniques from conscious breathing to meditation to visualization, but it seemed that no one was benefiting from these practices—at least in terms of improving his or her intuitive hits. My students were disappointed, but then I realized that none of them actually trusted their sense of self. The were trying, even with their eyes closed and deep breathing, more to impress me and get a good grade in the class, so to speak. They couldn't get out of their own way to perceive information from their own energy fields.

The ability to know that your perceptions are accurate has

to happen without others' validation. Intuition is not the result of diet, rituals, or wind chimes. It's the natural consequence of having self-esteem, the greatest power you can have. With self-esteem, your life can broaden into an adventure because you know in your gut that you can handle the unknown. And you can handle helping others without fear, which is true liberation.

The third chakra is the energy center of "you"—of the self. This is your ego-center, the power zone of your survival intuition. You live more from this third energy center than from all your other six chakras. Your perceptions in this energy field shift from "how you belong"—tribal perceptions of the first chakra—and the relationship exchanges of the second chakras— "to whom you belong"—to your personal, individual sense of identity.

Melissa J. described this difference perfectly when she wrote, "There are personal and impersonal acts of service. An impersonal act of service would be, say, actively participating on a Habitat for Humanity project. Personal acts of service are different. You decide to help a specific person in your life and thus exhibit godly behavior with authentic acts of service."

Melissa's comment by no means diminishes the value of volunteering on projects such as Habitat for Humanity, but indicates the importance of becoming empowered enough within ourselves so that we can empower another person. Helping to build a home for someone, a first-chakra act of power, is a way of helping others that has very tangible results. But the ability to build up another person's self-esteem, a quintessential third-chakra act of power, is less visible and usually more personally demanding. Helping to provide a home is transitional in its use of your energy and time, but helping to empower someone is transformational and may cost a lot more energetically. You can actually see the house you helped to build, but you cannot weigh or measure the influence you have had on enhancing someone's self-esteem. You can say, for instance, "I put that window in the south wall of this room," but you cannot truly justify a statement such as, "I'm the reason why he made something of himself."

Your own ego does desire to be recognized for any help that you give and it definitely can influence how and when you decide to help, and whether you ask for thanks or are content to remain anonymous. A woman I met was very bitter because she had volunteered to help a community by counseling its trauma victims, but felt cheated of recognition for her efforts by other volunteers. To volunteer means to help where needed and as necessary; but for this woman and many others, volunteering is a means to garner accolades and to establish a base of personal power and authority. Power plays and politics can be as common in volunteer organizations as they are in businesses, of course, and are quintessential third-chakra challenges.

On the other hand, I met an individual at one of my workshops who was refreshingly conscious and direct about what she can and cannot give. She said, "I don't make a good volunteer because I need to be the boss and volunteers can't ascend in the ranks the way I need to. And I'll admit, I need recognition for what I do because I do good work." Her response, by the way, does not indicate that she lacks a generous spirit but that she understands how to say, "Enough." People burn out constantly because they cannot manage their compassionate hearts; they have constant impulses to try to rescue others—and sometimes to try to control them. Coming to terms with our desire for recognition and our call to act generously—and invisibly—is a major task of our third energy center.

*   *   *

In charity there is no excess.

—SIR FRANCIS BACON,
OF GOODNESS, AND GOODNESS OF NATURE

Generosity is not *a* way of life, but *the* way of life. As the Buddha said, "Many garlands can be made from a heap of flowers. Many good deeds should be done by one born a mortal." Many of the great spiritual masters encourage people to give without strings attached—to do good just for the sake of doing good. Long before we get to the point of being able to provide higher, invisible acts of power, we need to provide visible ones. We need to delight in helping someone heal or in creating wonderful surprises for others. These are the means through which we discover the enchantment of giving as well as the gift of receiving.

Several people shared personal examples of physical gifts from invisible donors. One woman received a series of Christmas presents left anonymously at her door twenty-four days in a row; another woman found that the driver in a toll booth line ahead of her had paid her toll. In these and other such experiences of anonymous benefactors, the recipients reported that as a result, they felt as if they had had an experience of grace, which renewed their belief in the power of others' goodness. These simple, physical gifts conveyed life-changing effects.

On a more metaphysical level, one man wrote that when he was a teenager, he was headed in the wrong direction. He was in a broken home and had no one to care for him. One day after school, he went to a friend's house, hoping they would ask him to stay for dinner, as he knew that there would be no meal waiting for him at his home. "This family did invite me to stay for dinner, for which I was deeply grateful. But what really changed my life was that this was the first time I ever experienced a family praying together before a meal. I didn't know how to do that, so I just folded my hands and kept my head bowed. Then my friend's father said, 'Thank you, God, for bringing Billy to our table and into our family. Let him know that we would be very grateful if he would join us for dinner as often as he would like.' I started to weep. I never experienced such respect. I felt a force enter into my stomach which I will always believe was grace because from that moment on, I valued my own life."

The Consciousness of Your Third Chakra

The superior man, when resting in safety, does not forget that danger may come. When in a state of security he does not forget the possibility of ruin. When all is orderly, he does not forget that disorder may come. Thus his person is not endangered, and his States and all their clans are preserved.

— CONFUCIUS

The Hindu name for this third energy center means "city of the shining jewel," a metaphor for the beauty of the empowered self. In fact, the motto of this chakra could be, "Honor oneself." The Christian sacrament of confirmation and the Jewish bar or bas mitzvah represent the energy of this chakra. When we are confirmed in a faith, we are consciously accepting the power and maturity of our individual self. We declare our intention to be a conscious member of the community.

This chakra also contains the power of endurance, the ability to withstand and accept that which the universe metes out to us over the course of our lives and to help others endure that which they cannot change. At the first-chakra level, we accept the circumstances of our birth, our tribe, and our family circumstances—the package our life comes in. In this third chakra, we learn to accept the package our self comes in—looks, intelligence, talents—characteristics that comprise the personal as opposed to the tribal ego and the individual responsibilities that are presented to us as we make our way in the world. We confirm and affirm who we are.

The key word for the third chakra is *self,* a small word around which you build your entire world. The energy of the self can be used in many ways—from "selfish" to "self-starting" to "self-empowered." The self encompasses our external, public persona and the interior self of the soul. Our spiritual task in learning to manage this complex energy is to move from "self-consciousness" to "consciousness of the self," so that we bring our ego and spirit into balance; we come into our own.

The third chakra is the center of your gut instinct, the more familiar name for survival intuition. Here you can *physically* feel personal intuitive guidance. I've never seen anyone point to his first chakra when expressing feelings, but we often put a hand on our solar plexus when we say things like, "I just had this gut feeling that I should move," or, "I knew right away that I could trust that person because I felt safe." Your rational mind often collides with intuitive instructions in your third chakra. Logic may tell you, for instance, that picking up a hitchhiker is risky, but your intuition may strongly communicate that you "must" stop and that you'll be safe. Many of the regrets people express in their letters reflect exactly this struggle between the often cold, fear-based instructions of our logical mind and the softer directives that come from our intuition.

The lessons of your third chakra usually concern self-esteem. At this level of spiritual maturation, you learn to listen to your interior self over the intense influences of your external environment, including family, friends, and people in your social and professional arenas.

Once you know who you are, nothing can stop you.

— STEDMAN GRAHAM

Performing an invisible act of service for themselves is immensely uncomfortable for many people who are used to caring physically for others, particularly mothers, female heads of households, adult children with elderly parents who are ill, and people in the health professions. Many people sacrifice themselves for others, becoming exhausted, fatigued, or ill before they will accept the need to take care of themselves and make choices that are personally lifesaving, such as leaving a dysfunctional marriage or choosing to follow a different spiritual tradition. Yet to evolve into spiritual maturity, you must become conscious and effective about who you are and what you need spiritually as well as physically. You must bring together your self-esteem and intuition in order to act from your power.

To mature to a point from which we can act "invisibly," we undergo considerable confrontations with the self and our personal motivations. Frequently at my workshops I toss out the question, "How many of you recognize that you act in many parts of your life and in your relationships like a rescuer or a servant?" Hands fly up at the speed of light, complemented by troubled facial expressions that communicate feelings of pain, rejection, and a lack of appreciation. One woman pondered, "When, oh, when will I learn not to give everything to a man who could not care less about me? I'm tired of men not appreciating how much I do for them." Men and women can both feel the same anguish, of course, the consequence of having a hidden agenda for helping others. As this woman so poignantly points out, giving for the wrong reasons is emotionally and physically depleting—and serves no one. Developing personal power includes learning not to negotiate your self-worth for the sake of someone else or sell yourself short for a job.

After one of my seminars where I mentioned the importance of self-respect in being able to help someone else, a woman came up to me and said, "I know what you are talking about. I'm a model and that's a competitive field. This one girl joined a group of us for a shoot. She was particularly attractive and we all notice that about each other immediately. She was nervous and she asked me how she looked in this one outfit. She looked fabulous, but I couldn't bring myself to tell her that. Instead I told her that she didn't look her best. She was devastated. I immediately felt guilty that I had made her feel so bad about herself, yet I could not bring myself to repair the damage I had done. I just didn't have a strong enough ego to help her out."

The woman who told me this story was obviously attuned to her own intuition; she knew this other model was seeking approval, connection, and a boost to her confidence. But because of her own insecurities, this woman could not afford to open to her deeper intuitive capacity and actually sense or feel the novice's vulnerability. Rather, she responded out of her own competitive fear and added to the younger woman's fears.

At the opposite end of the spectrum is this letter from Jen D.: "I am in the process of a divorce. While I know that ending my marriage was what needed to happen in order for change and growth to occur it is still a frightening upheaval of my life.

"On the same day, I received two cards. One arrived in the mail and was from my mother. She and I are close in many ways, but my mother is not normally one for deep emotional conversation. In this note, she expressed how proud she was of me, and that she saw me as very brave for being willing to change my life. She acknowledged that she has watched me follow my passions in life and finds this inspirational. Reading her note touched me deeply and brought tears to my eyes. I've never felt so seen by her in my life. Her words gave me a new strength and lifted my spirits when I needed a boost.

"The second card was on my desk at work. It was from a coworker, a woman a good bit older than I. She had drawn a key in the card and written. 'This is the key to the rest of your life.' She went on to write that she believed in me and knew I had so much to offer. Again, I felt graced in an unexpected way. Her words meant the world to me at that moment. She gave me the gift of knowing I was not alone and that I was understood. Both these acts of service came as complete surprises. I now feel like I can do pretty much anything!"

Giving, Receiving, and the Private Agenda

Give what you have. To someone, it may be better than you dare to think.

— HENRY WADSWORTH LONGFELLOW

The ancient Greek philosopher Epictetus wrote, "The universe is but one great city, full of beloved ones, divine and human by nature, endeared to each other." Caring for other people is a cosmic obligation that we all share. We each are an individual fragment of a collective soul and are called to help each other, to live with a compassionate awareness of all of humanity.

Yet if giving and receiving were simple, people would not suffer such anxiety, guilt, and worry over these acts. Like the woman mentioned earlier who felt unappreciated for her volunteer efforts, we all must face the challenge of learning to offer our services and releasing the desire for recognition. One woman summed up the emotions of many, "It's not that I was seeking any thanks, but it sure would have been nice to receive some." True, but we have to come to terms with our personal agendas and desires while on the path of impersonal, spiritual service. Our task is to infuse our action with all our faith and belief in its goodness and release it into the universe to do its invisible work.

Of the many letters that reported gifts with no strings attached, Ruth H.'s is one of the loveliest: "Giving service to others is part of how I was raised. Not that it was lectured into me; it was an example shown by both my parents, scout leaders, distress center volunteers, helping neighbors, and colleagues. From the stories my dad used to tell, I know that he was raised that way, as well. His father was a policeman during the Depression, but also had a small hobby farm. With eight children, the farm was a necessity. Every Saturday morning, my dad and his older brother would take a pull-cart down the road and drop off eggs and vegetables to those who were having a tough time. No fanfare, not even a knock on the door. The food was just placed on the doorstep. I recently took a course on servant leadership. I have consciously tried to apply the principles at work ever since, asking myself in difficult situations, 'How can I serve this situation best?' I am motivated by a desire to ease the burden of others, to let them know they are not alone in their struggles."

Thomas Merton, the renowned Catholic mystic, wrote a book entitled *No Man Is an Island*, which I consider a type of theology for the third chakra. Merton explores the spiritual dilemma of how we must learn to love ourselves—another way of saying we must develop self-esteem—before we can truly give freely or invisibly to others. He brilliantly describes the challenge of awakening to the realization that to care for yourself as much as you care for others is also a way of serving others. In fact, ultimately you cannot genuinely care for someone else—free of any private agendas—unless you hold yourself in equal and loving regard. Merton writes:

We cannot love ourselves unless we love others, and we cannot love others unless we love ourselves. But a selfish love of ourselves makes us incapable of loving others. The difficulty of this commandment lies in the paradox that it would have us love ourselves unselfishly, because even our love of ourselves is something we owe others.

What do I mean by loving ourselves properly? I mean, first of all, desiring to live, accepting life as a very great gift and a great good, not because of what it gives us, but because of what it enables us to give to others.

But if we live for others, we will gradually discover that no one expects us to be "as gods." We will see that we are human, like everyone else, that we all have weaknesses and deficiencies, and that these limitations of ours play a most important part in all our lives. It is because of them that we need others and others need us. We are not all weak in the same spots, and so we supplement and complete one another, each one making up in himself for the lack in another. Only when we see ourselves in our true human context, as members of a race which is intended to be one organism and "one body," will we begin to understand the positive importance not only of the successes but of the failures and accidents in our lives.

While I have never come across someone who is terminally ill as a result of overgiving, many people do suffer from anger, resentment, and jealousy when their efforts go unnoticed. Third-chakra distresses are immediately palpable; there is nothing subtle about the responses from a hurt or rejected ego. Your solar plexus is a highly sensitive energy zone, doubly so because it is also the center of your survival intuition. You can energetically hemorrhage as a result of giving too much of yourself or giving for the wrong reasons. Conditions like depression, emotional exhaustion, or chronic pain can develop as a result of rescuer fatigue. Becoming conscious of your self, aware of who you are and what you can and cannot do, is one of the important tasks of spiritual maturity and the hero's journey.

Grace for the Self

We do not believe in ourselves until someone reveals that deep inside us is valuable, worth listening to, worthy of our trust, sacred to our touch. Once we believe in ourselves we can risk curiosity, wonder, spontaneous delight or any experience that reveals the human spirit.

—E. E. CUMMINGS

Birthing the self is an archetypal struggle that awaits every individual. We must go it alone on our own hero's journey to discover our individual spiritual resources. But sometimes we need inspiration and support—especially at the beginning of our journey. In many of the letters I received, people shared their third-chakra experiences in which they felt they had been empowered. Some of them had taken place years ago, and yet their healing and transformational effects continue to be profound. These letters are beautiful witnesses to how little it takes to empower someone's spirit.

Lisa M. shared, "My roommate is an absolute, self-admitted 'princess.' If there's any caretaking, it's generally me that is the caregiver. She is absentminded, self-absorbed, and forgets everything that is happening in my life. But I love her dearly and she is my best friend. And when it really counts, she is always there for me. Earlier this year, I was particularly sad and depressed over the break-up of a relationship. All my possessions were in storage and I was living with my friend until I decided what my next steps would be. It was the worst winter in history with tons of snow everywhere. I owned seven snow scrapers, but they were all in storage and I was just depressed enough to be perfectly stubborn about the whole thing. I'd just use my arms to clear the snow off the car. Anyway, one day, when I was as low as I could be, I went out to my car and the snow was scraped off—all of it. It was the princess! Every day, she had my car cleaned off before I left for work. This was a miraculous and strange feeling for me. She convinced me to go see her shrink and look into antidepressants. Well, I went. No drugs required—this therapist gave me a simple gift, a way to look at things that completely altered the way I felt about myself and my situation. I laughingly called her the Princess Marilyn snow brusher, to which she said, 'Well, when you notice the snow still on your car in the morning, chances are you're getting better.' And sure enough, as the weeks passed, the princess simply left the snow scraper on the car, then left it leaning against the car, and then no snow scraper at all. I was cured. This was the nicest thing anyone ever did for me."

Sometimes, empowering another requires a kind of tough love. When the desire to help is genuine, tough choices serve both the giver and the receiver, as Haven I. succinctly described in her letter: "While I was in my midtwenties and going through another relationship with an unavailable man, I found myself— yet again—in a 'high drama' state and calling upon my closest and undoubtedly wisest friend, Lyn. She had been there to comfort me always. This time she said, 'I am busy. I have a lot going on. I don't have time for you.' She set up a boundary. I cried and cried myself to sleep that night. Where were the answers? Where was the advice I needed? Now I feel fairly ridiculous about the whole debacle with that man. The answers to who I was and a sense of comfort was all inside of me. Lyn could not have shown more love for me in any other way. It was the largest push I have ever received in learning how to listen and understand myself."

Let me add that men certainly have not been spared from giving too much for the wrong reasons to the wrong women. This is a common behavior that comes from the fear of being alone—a core fear of your third chakra.

Another tough-love gift is shared in this letter from Kathleen K., a nurse who writes, "I was at the lowest time in my life. My marriage of seventeen years had failed, my seventeen-year-old son had been killed in an accident, and I was about to lose my job. I was called in to the director of nurses' office. She had no reason to support me or do anything but fire me. I deserved to be fired and could have lost my nurse's license that day, which, in my eyes, would have made my failure complete as a human being on this earth. All the evidence against me was presented and I had no defense. I was guilty, totally humiliated, and felt like I had failed myself and my profession. She looked at me with such compassion and said, 'Kathleen, I'm going to believe in you until you can believe in yourself.' She let me keep my job. She gave me resources and support. She became my mentor and friend. I never understood how or why or what motivated her on that day, but I believe that in that simple moment, she changed my path. She started me on my journey back to believing in myself."

> *No one can make you feel inferior without your consent.*
>
> —ELEANOR ROOSEVELT

After having read through all the tender stories that people sent me, I will never believe that there is nothing we can do. There is *always* something we can do for another if we get out of the frame of mind that size, quantity, and outcome determines the value of what we have to give another. This is especially true, I believe, when it comes to enhancing someone's self-esteem. Healing emotional wounds can require years of psychological effort and counseling. Yet the simplest kindness can have more effect on a person's well-being than months and months of therapy. Perhaps this is because interactions with each other are where the power is. The experience described by this letter's author is critical to the third chakra: personal security and self-esteem.

Writes Malynda L.: "Nine years ago, I was working in a health food store and going to school for business and naturopathy. One of my regular customers came in and gave me a large manila envelope. She said someone she knew had asked her to give it to me. I of course was not making enough money and was relying on school loans to make ends meet. This woman handed me the envelope and left very fast. I opened it up and inside was a beautiful note reminding me that I was doing a great job. I was obviously doing the right work with the ND education, that I had a lot to offer and that had helped her on numerous occasions. She wrote that she was proud of me and wanted to let me know that all the hard work was not going unnoticed. At the time, I really needed to know it. Inside the envelope along with the note was a crisp hundred-dollar bill. I was stunned. I was just doing and being who I am, but the effect of her appreciation was much more than words can describe. It was just the boost to my ego, my mind, and my heart that I needed."

The Courage to Act

You must give some time to your fellow men. Even if it's a little thing, do something for others—something for which you get no pay but the privilege of doing it.

—ALBERT SCHWEITZER

Courage is harbored in the third chakra. At some point on our hero's journey, we will have to risk our personal safety and accept the consequences of our actions. The men and women in our armed forces do this every day, as do many people in health services who treat patients with contagious diseases.

A few years ago while teaching in South Africa, I met a gentleman who had left his medical practice in his hometown of Amsterdam to do volunteer work in Africa for people with AIDS. He had left home at age thirty-one because he had felt a call to serve where he would be needed. His family was greatly opposed to the idea, not only because he was going to a politically unsettled area, but because he was working every day with a chronic, usually fatal disease. But he deeply believed that with his personal and spiritual call to serve, a special grace of protection had been included in his Sacred Contract. He remarked that, "If God wanted me dead, he would not have to bother sending me all the way to South Africa. He could just as easily have arranged an accident in Amsterdam to save me the price of a plane ticket."

I marveled at his devotion and humility. He was not obviously trying to imitate Albert Schweitzer or Mother Teresa, but he had the same special quality of energy as they did that was healing and comforting.

Sometimes, of course, the call to help others *will* expose you to danger. Remember that Jesus himself didn't guarantee a smooth way or a peaceful life for his disciples. Altruistic rescuers who have tried to save drowning people have themselves been drowned; medics and pastors are killed in wars just as the soldiers they serve are. And of course military personnel are killed as they perform their duties in a "just" war as well as in an "unjust" war. These tragedies make us question the fairness and compassion of the universe since these people didn't deserve to die. But I maintain that we have to extract from our vocabulary the word *deserve*, a third-chakra word that does nothing but cause suffering. Too many people resent other people's good fortune and resent their own lives and family because they feel they haven't gotten what they deserve. Job lamented to God that he didn't deserve the suffering he was sent, but redeemed himself in the end by trusting that a wisdom much greater than his was working behind the scenes of his life.

Where you fall, there your God pushed you down.
— NIGERIAN PROVERB

Let's say you have been blessed with a brilliant idea that you passionately wanted to follow but you needed an enormous amount of help to bring your dream to fruition. Let's say that heaven sent an unconventional solution—a stranger with no references, lawyer, or contracts. Could you enter into an agreement under such conditions? You might, if you knew how to read your intuitive signals clearly and had the courage of your convictions. The author of the following letter, Forester D., remains grateful because a stranger came along and decided, just like that, to support his dream of opening a fitness studio.

After Forester started his personal training business, he wasn't getting enough clients, so to keep it going, he remortgaged his house twice, "And then sold the house, sold my truck and my furniture. Mostly, I puzzled why more people weren't signing up for a healthier beginning in my beautiful studio. I spent about fifteen thousand dollars on ads and then I thought, 'Bigger must be the answer.' So I moved to a busier part of town, tripled the size of my space, and leased more equipment. Do I need to tell you how my stomach [third chakra] felt through all this? Here I am, with a $175,000 lease and triple the operating costs. I started to wonder why I would insist on having the highest national certification, compassion for the 'unfit,' a spectacular studio with private showers and 'light therapy,' color-coordinated upholstery, a kitchen to make healthy soup—and doing this all by myself, clocking in fourteen- to sixteen-hour days."

Eventually, Forester had to face his losses. "I called my vendors to talk about lease fulfillment. I called the bank to see how to avoid bankruptcy and I called my accountant. And then I called my dear friend E. Lotz, who had found the beautiful location I would now have to leave. I guess I called E. because her name had a particularly funny resonance to it that day: E. Lotz . . . lots . . . hmm. I told her I was giving up. 'Oh,' she said, 'let's not do that just yet. Let me make a call first. In about three hours, I got a call from a woman whose last name was Powers-Keyes who said that she had been interested in opening a fitness studio for adult women. We immediately clicked and now have a partnership. The studio is saved, and in so many ways, so am I and so is she."

Just think for one moment about all the cosmic choreography that had to take place for this dream to incarnate. What if one of them had been too afraid to act with the extraordinary speed of intuition, preferring to hoof it at the speed of logic, paperwork, and fear? The investor obviously had a deep enough belief in her own power and vision not to run from an opportunity that was for her as much an intervention of grace as her saving Forester's fitness center was for him. Forester ended his e-mail with an inspiring paragraph about how he sees his mission of healing and inspiring others:

> Clear vision: You promise to pursue your goal by honoring your journey with the integrity of your word. Believe in the power of your ability to perceive a goal, and then your way to that goal, even through the difficult parts. Commend your efforts. Rewards are earned by those with the vision to see beyond the temporary. Promise to honor your journey here together as we embrace the benefits of a productive and mindful plan. Your capacity is limited only by your ability to believe change is possible.

Heaven gives you chances to see how much of your spirit remains imprisoned by yesterday's choices and consequences. Your
intuition can help you transcend the fog of tribal programming
and assess people and situations in the present, unhampered by
past, outmoded associations and beliefs. Your mind will produce
reasons, emotional scar tissue, a litany of your personal history's
positive and negative experiences, while your intuitive sense will
evaluate the energy of the moment. Ultimately, you want to treat
each opportunity as a potential new beginning. This will come
from a strong sense of self and spirit in balance—self-respect—
and give you the courage to move ahead.

*Security is mostly a superstition. It does not exist in nature. . . . Life is
either a daring adventure or nothing.*

—HELEN KELLER

Courage affects what we are willing to do for ourselves as well
as what we are willing to do for another person. Many times we
find ourselves in situations in which reaching out to another person challenges the rule or will of the tribe. In these experiences,
we have to decide whether we have the courage to act on a personal intuitive hit or whether we repress that guidance out of fear
of tribal judgment or ridicule. One woman shared exactly this
type of experience and demonstrates that even the smallest act
of service or compassion takes courage. She also shows the consequences of courageous choices, whether professional or personal, live on forever.

Writes K.: "I am a female police sergeant and this experience
happened to me when I was twenty-three years old and a new police officer. I was working a midnight shift and it was cold out. A
veteran officer and I were sent to a vacant field to meet with two
homeless people and fire department paramedics. The woman

was not feeling well and I found a shelter for her, but the shelter did not accept men, and they wanted to stay together. I did not know what else to do, so I gave the man a dollar and a quarter. I sent them to the all-night restaurant where they both could drink coffee for a dollar and I told him to use the quarter to call me if her condition got worse. The homeless people headed for the restaurant and the veteran officer chewed me out for giving money away. He asked me if I was going to give money to every homeless person. I left thinking that I had really mishandled the situation.

"Months later, I was on a different shift and officers were calling for additional officers in reference to a man fighting. When I got there, I noticed it was the same homeless man. When this man saw me, he stopped resisting. When the arresting officers got him to the police department, they put him in the holding cells. The man became loud and disorderly, but when he saw me, he stopped. I did not connect his behavior change to my presence until another officer asked him about it and he told the officer about the dollar and a quarter I had given to him. When I was driving him to the county jail, I asked him why he was an alcoholic and he told me that he lived in New York with his wife, who was a nurse. He said that she was on her way home from work and some kids threw a brick at her car. The brick hit her windshield and she died in the car crash. He was an electrician, but after that experience, he became an alcoholic. The last time I heard anything about him, he sent a message to me through another officer that he had met. He wanted me to know that he was living in an apartment now and working as an electrician again. Whenever I think of his story, I always think of that saying, 'Except for the grace of God go I,' and I've learned that in life, kindness matters."

Melissa F. wrote about facing her fear of homeless people, which was rooted in a lack of personal comfort: "Beggars have been a perplexing challenge to me. I used to give change away a lot but after a few bad experiences eventually I started feeling 'taken.' Then I went through a period where I was straight-out nasty to them and would tell them to leave me alone pretty rudely before they could even start their speech. I was mean to one of them in front of a friend, who buffered my nasty remarks and gave the guy some change. Once he left, she told me he was from a shelter that made them go out and ask for donations to earn their place to sleep. I felt like a chump for being rude to some poor guy that was just trying to make sure he could sleep inside that night. I started to see that I was being rude because my financial situation was keeping me just a breath away from his. I was scared of becoming a beggar myself and was nasty to all of them as if I was trying to bark at my own fear of total poverty. Now I politely tell them I can't help or I give them a little if I can. I also send them a prayer in my mind and wish them well."

To free us from the expectations of others, to give us back to ourselves—there lies the great, singular power of self-respect.

—JOAN DIDION

Our fear of others' opinions can be a very real controlling force. Many people repress their intuitive guidance for fear of how others will judge them. In the following letter, Matthew G. had to find the courage in himself to help another person, even while imagining what "they" might be thinking: "I was leaving school one night, walking down the street towards the gym and silently praying (though not obviously because I'm not one to pray—I just talk to myself and hope things get better) and wishing that an opportunity would come my way that would let me prove my worth as a decent person.

"About one minute later, I saw a man coming my way with his head down, staggering a little, and it looked as if his legs were about to give out from under him. He didn't look obviously homeless so I thought that perhaps he was just sick. I kept watching him anyway because I was concerned. He started to walk toward the scaffolding we were walking under and I saw him grab hold of it to keep himself up. I stopped to see if he was okay. He said he was and I stayed with him for a few seconds to make sure. It seemed that he wasn't going to make it to where he was going so I decided to stay with him until he got his bearings. He was very friendly after he got himself somewhat together, but he also was obviously very drunk. We struck up a conversation. He started telling me how he was planning on killing himself that very night. I couldn't believe what I was hearing. Do you know what it's like to hear those words? All of a sudden I felt responsible for saving this man's life. I walked with him and asked him where I could take him. He mentioned just a few streets ahead as he put his arm through mine as if he was my prom date. I was a little uncomfortable to be walking like this, to say the least.

"I knew there was a shelter a few blocks up so I decided I'd walk with him there and then go on my way. I didn't know how far I was willing to go with this guy or how much I was willing to commit to him. I just knew that I couldn't leave him alone at that moment. We began to walk and he was in good spirits, talking away and obviously very happy for my company, telling me about himself and how nice I was for stopping to help him, adding that he's not usually like this and that he is a good person. I knew that he was because somehow I could feel what was inside his heart. He really touched me and he was a very charming guy. In fact, he was more charming and friendly than a lot of my own friends. I told him that things were okay and that there are good things in this world to live for and that obviously God didn't want him to take his own life that night because he met someone like me who gave him some hope.

"I heard people laughing at us as we walked by—me, a normal, perhaps yuppie-looking fellow walking arm-in-arm with a disheveled homeless guy who reeked of gin. I used to let those people bother me and that did start to, but for some reason on this night, I decided to let it slide. I realized, though perhaps sub-consciously, that what I had just asked for two minutes prior to meeting this man was just what was handed to me at this mo-ment—an opportunity to do good in this life on the deepest and most meaningful of levels—to really reach out to someone who needed help. I walked him to the corner and he sat down and lit a cigarette. He was all smiles by then and I decided to leave, though I didn't feel that good about it because, after all, he did say he was going to kill himself. But he seemed much better and I didn't know what else to do. He didn't let me go without a big hug and I could feel the eyes of other commuters on us and I felt even more embarrassed. But you know what? I had to do what was right at that moment. As much as he though I helped him, he really helped me. I hope he knows that and I did try and tell him so. He gave me the chance to be a better person for once in my life and to reach out to someone who needed it. That was as great a gift as what he perceived I gave him."

The Power of the Simple Gift

I expect to pass through this world but once; any good thing therefore that I can do, any kindness that I can show to any fellow creature, let me do it now; let me not defer to neglect it, for I shall not pass this way again.

—ETIENNE DE GRELLET

The alchemist in me loves to see the myriad ways in which the universe "multiplies the fishes and the loaves." You don't need something great or huge to change the quality of your life. A seed for transformation exists within the soul of each act of goodness. Faith, patience, endurance, and respect are also the central energies of your third chakra and those that help you discern what you need to do. All of us at one point or another have questioned our ability to make a difference, but the following letter from Scott L. is a tribute to a simple act that triggered the alchemical power of transformation.

Writes Scott, "My story is about my neighbor Phil M. He is a most unusual man, although he would never see it that way. In fact, I think he is part of a species that no longer exists. He is the most unselfish person I think I've ever had the privilege of knowing. I first met him when I moved into the house next door. He was a janitor and worked nights, an unassuming, nice, and gentle guy. One day I needed help fixing a leak in the bathtub. He invited me inside. He had the most unbelievable collection of books, from Roman history to Nietzsche to Schopenhauer to Dickens; you name it, he had it. All of his walls contained bookshelves full of great novels. I remember feeling stupid for judging him because he was a janitor. He told me that he had 160 hours of English literature but never graduated from college.

"Anytime I needed anything, he offered to help. He helped me put my roof on, my deck, build my greenhouse, and build my gardens. His generosity knew no end for those who needed his assistance. Because of his help, we transformed our house, which was a dump, into a place we could sell and consequently move to a bigger house. He would never let us pay him back either. Once in a while we'd pay a vet bill for his cat or buy him chocolate. But we never got close to paying him back.

"As I got to know him, I learned he had a very tough upbringing. His father was an alcoholic and beat him and his brothers. Phil came away more intact than his brothers. He made a conscious effort to be positive and supportive when he had many reasons to be negative and quit. He took care of Margie, a woman who had been in a wheelchair for fifty years. He was the main reason she never had to go to a nursing home during the last years of her life. In the last months of her life, he left his job in order to take her to the hospital.

"Shortly after I met him, his best friend died. His widow had no money so Phil paid for his funeral with the money his dad left him when he died the year before. He gave his friend's widow money to move across the country so she could live with her family. His father's inheritance was completely gone after that. When he moved out of his house to live with Marge as a caregiver, I noticed an electronic piano in his room. I asked if he ever played it. He said, 'Oh, yes,' and then he sat down and started to play Chopin. Chopin! I said that in seven years, I had never heard him practice . . . he replied that he played late at night after work wearing earphones so as not to wake us up. Our houses were very close together.

"There are many stories like that of Phil giving his time and energy to others. He asks for nothing in return from anyone. He is just a decent person. He is not caught up in trying to make a grand gesture with his life. He does not have a lot of friends, spends a lot of time alone, and yet, without him, my life, Margie's life, and others would be so different. He would be mortified to know I was writing about him as he is a very private person. He lives simply and does his best to make his way each day. He has no money, no real family. When Margie died a couple of months ago, he had nowhere to go. He made a comment about moving into a run-down apartment complex close to downtown. Amy and I asked him if he would move in to the lower level of our new home. We could not imagine him living like that after what he has done for others. He lives with us now and is welcome to stay as long as he wants. We live across the street from a junior college. Maybe he will finish his studies there. In my previous life I would never have associated with someone like Phil. Now I can't imagine what my life would have been like had he not been my neighbor. He showed me that you don't have to do great things in life to have a worthwhile life and that by the simple act of unselfishly giving to others you can make a huge difference with your own life. I have truly been blessed by God to know such a man."

The story of Phil W. reminds me of the meaning of "Chop wood and carry water," the Zen teaching that attention to our actions holds the real energy of grace, the true meaning of an invisible act of power.

Examining the Heart of
Your Third Chakra

Hidden within any kindness that someone does for you is a new beginning for your life. Every good act, word, or deed is a catalyst for a chain reaction. As we become more mindful of the power of our intuition, we will become more mindful of others.

The examination of your third chakra leads you into the examination of your self and the courage that determines the choices you make. Ask yourself:

As the Giver:
1. Do I need recognition for what I do for others?
2. Do others' opinions influence what I do for myself or other people?
3. Am I afraid to take a risk on behalf of another person?

4. Would I resent being forgotten by someone I once did a favor for?
5. Is it difficult for me to encourage or empower another person?
6. Do I withhold approval for others deliberately because I fear they will grow in self-esteem and I will suffer as a result?

As the Receiver:
1. Do I find asking for help humiliating?
2. Do I sometimes think that what others do for me isn't enough?
3. Am I presently in a vulnerable circumstance?

A THIRD-CHAKRA PRAYER

I release into this universe my trust that my journey in life and all who walk my path with me are there by divine design. Therefore, I trust that along this path, others will always be there for me, even when I cannot see them waiting for me. And I open myself to be of service to those who may provide me the gift of empowerment.

THE PRAYER OF THOMAS MERTON
Dear God, I have no idea where I am going.
I do not see the road ahead of me.
I cannot know for certain where it will end.
Nor do I really know myself . . . and the fact that I think that
    I am following Your will does not mean that I am
    actually doing so.
But I believe this:
I believe that the desire to please You does in fact please You.
I hope I have that desire in everything I do.

I hope I never persist in anything apart from that desire.
And I know that if I do this You will lead me by the right
road, though I may know nothing about it at the time.
Therefore I will trust You always, for though I may be lost—
and in the shadow of death—I will not be afraid, because
I know You will never leave me to face my troubles all
alone.

CHAPTER 4

Gifts of the Heart

Love cannot remain by itself—it has no meaning. Love has to be put into action and that action is service. How do we put the love for God in action? By being faithful to our family. And to the duties that God has entrusted to us. Whatever form we are, able or disabled, rich or poor, it is not how much we do but how much love we put in the doing—a lifelong sharing of love with others.
— MOTHER TERESA, *LOVE SEEKS TO SERVE*

A man in one of my workshops took me aside to tell me the story of his divorce. It remains unique in my experience. This man told me that his wife found his compassion for others impossible to live with. As he told me, "My ex-wife believes that people should take care of themselves. I have always believed people should care for other people. We would actually argue over my desire to make up Christmas gift boxes for families or donate money and it wasn't because we didn't have enough ourselves. We could have been millionaires and my desire to help others would still have bothered her. She simply wasn't ready to care for anyone or anything more than herself and it was better for both of us to go our separate ways." This man's ex-wife didn't like his style of love, his open heart. She was so frightened by life in general, so invested in the myth that there isn't enough to go around, and so scared of her own vulnerabilities that she kept at

arm's length virtually anyone who might break through her fragile emotional wall.

Love is simple, but it's not easy.

A common misconception about love is that in order to have
it we need another individual on whom to focus it; we need a tar-
get, an object, a recipient. But the spiritual masters of all the
world religions show us that it is possible simply to learn how to
love—without a reason, without a person. Jesus said, for instance, "If you love those who love you, what reward will you
get? Do not even the tax collectors do as much? . . . You must
therefore set no bounds to your love, just as your heavenly Father sets none to his" (Matt. 5:43–48). And a more contemporary
spiritual teacher, Antoine de Saint-Exupery, the author of *The
Little Prince*, notes, "Love is not thinking, but being."

> *Where love rules, there is no will to power; and where power
> predominates, there love is lacking. The one is the shadow of the other.*
>
> —CARL JUNG

Heart intuition—love—is a greater force than survival intuition, the power of your first three chakras. At this fourth level,
we move out of the physical and into spiritual territory. This
fourth energy center draws you into depths of feeling, and not
just personal feelings for people—family, friends, colleagues—
already involved in your life. Love, after all, influences everything, and it expands your capacity to intuit other people's
vulnerabilities and needs and be open to helping them. Love for
humanity is a central motivating force behind many acts of service and gives the strength to sustain months or even years of
commitment. This same sacred force draws to you those who are
able to offer you that quality of service, too, as you'll see in some
of the letters in this chapter.

Even when we can see into the heart of someone's needs, however, we are not all willing or able to help. Many people cannot give more than basic physical assistance—food, shelter, money—that characterizes the generosity of the first three chakras. This kind of generosity is vital, for hunger imprisons the body and the spirit and limits the freedom of the soul. Yet becoming spiritually mature means that we develop the consciousness and power to move beyond that physical comfort zone—from the impersonal, although vital, actions of donating goods to acts of spiritual empowerment.

The following letter captures the essence of the difference— and the distance—between third-chakra survival intuition and fourth-chakra heart intuition.

Writes Michael W., "One evening in San Francisco, I walked along Van Ness Avenue among the usual assortment of people: young couples hand-in-hand, a few older people either alone or in couples, and of course the homeless out panhandling. I was heading towards a popular place where I planned to have dinner. As I neared the corner next to the restaurant's entrance, I saw two homeless men. One was middle-aged, sitting on the pavement with his back against a mailbox. He looked filthy dirty. His face, his black-gray hair, and his beard were lined with dried sweat and dirt. His clothes were old and blackened with dirt and filth. Under his thick eyebrows, his eyes appeared glazed, unfocused, as if his mind was in another world. From his speech—babbling and incoherent—I gathered that he was in another world or perhaps schizophrenic, I thought as I matched his eyes and mumblings to patients I'd seen working in a state psychiatric hospital.

"In front of the entrance stood an older man, also in old clothes, but his were only moderately dirty, and he appeared calm and coherent. He knew where he was and exactly what he was doing. As I approached the restaurant entrance, a young, very attractive couple walked out of the door. They were handsome and well dressed, looking very happy, intelligent, and affluent. The beautiful young woman held a white Styrofoam take-out box in her hand. The older man stepped up to them, saying, 'Money for food?' At that instant, I darted past them, thus avoiding having to deal with the panhandling. As I entered the restaurant the young woman extended the take-out box to the older man who immediately took the box and said very graciously, 'Thank you, thank you. God bless you.' I turned to look because offering and accepting the food was not what I had expected would happen. The older man smiled at the couple then turned toward the mailbox, where the middle-aged man was sitting. He opened the box. There was half a meal in it along with a plastic knife and fork. The older man used the knife to cut off the top of the box; then he carefully placed it on the mailbox. He then pushed half the food into the box top and placing the fork next to the food, the older man bent down to the other man and held the food in front of him. Very gently he said, 'Here, brother, have something to eat.'

"The middle-aged man looked up dimly. He seemed only vaguely aware that someone was talking to him. The older man spoke again, very kindly, saying, 'C'mon, brother, here's some food.' From far away, this man slowly began to come back. His eyes started to partially focus. He looked confused as he inhaled the smell of food that was right in front of his face. Slowly he came back into this world, able to understand that someone was offering him food. The older man waited patiently. Finally, when the middle-aged man seemed to understand, the older man said, "C'mon brother, have something to eat.' Numbly, the middle-aged man took the food, muttered, 'Thanks,' and slowly found the fork and began to eat. The older man picked up the other half of the box of food, sat down next to the middle-aged man, and together they began to eat."

The homeless man's compassion and respect for someone

worse off than himself is exquisite. When you realize that another person is starving for a serving of dignity, would you be able to walk away from him or her having done nothing? If your spiritual wiring is in any kind of working order, the answer is, no, of course, you wouldn't. I am not suggesting that this means you fill the man's pantry and pockets, but you would be called to do something by your ability to see into the heart of his needs and sense that his hunger is also spiritual.

Michael's contrite letter reveals the internal conflict created when the heart does not override our survival instinct's fears. The writer was clear from the beginning that his heart would not make an emotional connection with these two homeless men. Yet the heart contact between the two men obviously left its mark on his conscience, or he would not have taken the time to write this letter. Had Michael paused at the door of the restaurant and responded to the request with compassion and without fear, that show of respect would have been a supreme act of service. Food with dignity provides physical as well as spiritual sustenance.

Michael is at a breaking point, or a "breakthrough" point. He is dancing around his fourth chakra and attempting to quell his guilt by writing a letter admitting to it, which is a fine exercise—once. But I can promise him—and you—that working through emotions with a pen will never work twice. Next time, his heart will force his identification with his homeless soul mates—and not let him dodge a fourth-chakra connection out of fear.

I am very impressed by the willingness of the writers of all the letters I received to examine where they feel they could have acted better, more compassionately, more humanely. Their stories show an open heart and the courage to look honestly at themselves and what held them back from taking action. In this chapter, we will examine our own fear of making emotional connections. It's certainly an age-old challenge, as we see from the following Grimm fairy tale of the old man and his grandson. We all tend to want sometimes to turn away from the weak and the frail, especially people who remind us of our own potential for illness and decline.

There once was a very old man, whose eyes had become dim, his ears dull of hearing, his knees trembled, and when he sat at the table he could hardly hold the spoon, and spilt the broth on the table cloth or let it run out of his mouth. His son and his son's wife were disgusted at this, so the old grandfather at last was made to sit in the corner behind the stove, and they gave him his food in an earthenware bowl, and not even enough of it. He used to look towards the table with his eyes full of tears. Once, his trembling hands could not hold the bowl, and it fell to the ground and broke. The young wife scolded him, but he said nothing and only sighed. Then they bought him a wooden bowl for a few halfpence, out of which he had to eat.

They were all once sitting when the little grandson of four years old began to gather together some bits of wood upon the ground. "What are you doing there?" asked the father. "I am making a little trough," answered the child, "for father and mother to eat out of when I am big."

The man and his wife looked at each other for a while and presently began to cry. Then they took the old grandfather to the table and henceforth always let him eat with them and likewise said nothing if he did spill a little.

I see something of God each hour of the
    Twenty-four, and each moment then,
In the faces of men and women I see God, and in
    My own face in the glass,
I find letters from God dropt in the street and every
    One is signed by God's name.

— WALT WHITMAN, "SONG OF MYSELF"

The Consciousness of Your Fourth Chakra

Can there be love which does not make demands on its object?

— CONFUCIUS

The physical anatomy of the human heart is wonderfully emblematic of our physical evolution as well as our spiritual evolution. The fetal heart goes through four definite stages, each becoming more complex, more human. In the first developmental stage, the fetal heart is like a tube and resembles a fish heart. In the next stage, it divides into two chambers and resembles a frog's heart. It then grows into three chambers, which is typical of reptiles such as snakes or turtles. In its final stage, it develops into the familiar four chambers typical of warm-blooded mammals' and the human heart—at the fourth level of power.

It takes courage to become a warm-blooded, fourth-chakra intuitive. We grow into a full heart, some faster than others. Very few people are born brimming with compassion, generosity, and a burning desire to do good for others. We incarnate with the potential to be that way, but to realize that potential we need nurturing, teachers, mentors, role models, and a belief in our own ability to survive in this world.

As we mature, we also develop an increasingly sophisticated view of God. Most people first envision God as a protective, punishing, and vengeful force. We invoke God to protect our family, our loved ones, and even our belongings—all first-, second-, and third-chakra concerns. We call on God to help us survive and avenge us when we're wronged. Initially, ours is a God of stuff. Even our prayers and rituals reflect this desire for "stuff protection." We pray, "God bless my stuff, please give me more stuff,

watch over me and my stuff, over my tribe, my partner, my business, my money; make me successful and secure." When we are
disappointed, our knee-jerk response is often, "Why isn't God
helping me?" or, for those who prefer a little more drama, "Why
am I being punished?"

When you begin to see your life symbolically and examine your
spiritual purpose, you begin to transition out of a "God-fearing"
life and into more of an interior, spiritual life. Your intuitive and
spiritual stamina begins to expand.

The key word for the fourth chakra is, not surprisingly, *love*,
although that word hardly summarizes the full magnitude of this
power center. In the Hindu tradition, the fourth chakra is the energy of the pure sound of creation. Your own consciousness of
people in need and your response to them also has the primal energy of an act of creation—you steady their spirits, give them the
faith to continue, and jump-start a new beginning in their life.
Love for your life, work, family, and friends also catalyzes creative juices and new opportunities.

In making heart contact with another person, we acknowledge the presence of God within that individual. The fourth
chakra is the true center of power within your energy anatomy;
it's the physical center of your spiritual and physical being. We
can take as our motto for this chakra "Love is divine power."

> *The meeting of two personalities is like the contact of two chemical*
> *substances: if there is any reaction, both are transformed.*
>
> —CARL G. JUNG

A letter written by Jack Z. beautifully describes fourth-chakra
intuition in action: "I have many special and magical memories

about my father. One of my favorites was the way he was so silently generous. He never made a public display of what he did for others. He simply did endless good and generous things, teaching me among other wise lessons, that life can be lived as a prayer in action. Every Thanksgiving, for example, he would put some money in an envelope and give it to my uncle, who owned a grocery store. He told my uncle to fill a basket with all the essentials for a Thanksgiving meal and then find a family in need and give it to them. He never wanted those families to know that he was their Thanksgiving angel. I have kept up that tradition out of my love for my dad, and also because I believe that we have to share our abundance with others. But this one Thanksgiving, for whatever reasons, I forgot this ritual. Thanksgiving came and went, and it wasn't until two days later that I realized that I had forgotten this tradition. I actually panicked because I felt that I had let my dad down and had broken our long-running tradition. In the privacy of my heart, I sent a message to my dad through my thoughts, asking him what I should do. Later that same day, I saw a man staring at a train in a toy shop window that was all decorated for Christmas. I just knew in my gut that he was wishing he could buy that for his son. I went into the store and purchased the train for this man. I sent the check out clerk outside to invite the man into the store, where he learned that "someone" had wanted him to have that train. He was stunned—absolutely stunned. He kept saying, 'But who . . . who would do this? My son wanted this train so badly. Who did this for me?' I left the store so filled with the spirit of my father and with gratitude that he had taught me so well."

Fourth-chakra intuition allows you to sense another person's emotional health. Your heart and energy help you become open to a spiritual problem that is disguised as a physical crisis. A fourth-chakra response to a financial crisis, for instance, would be intimately compassionate in its feeling, as opposed to a second-chakra response, which would be to help someone because it's the right, ethical thing to do. Both responses are spiritually and emotionally motivated, but you can feel the difference.

Once when I was in London I was approached by a young man from Finland who was very upset, having just missed his bus to the airport. His English was poor (mind you, my Finnish is nonexistent) and he was so frightened about missing his flight. He was crying and I could tell it was very difficult for him to ask for help. I had a heartfelt response to his situation—he reminded me of my nephew—so I waved down a taxi, gave him a hundred dollars, and told the driver to take him to the airport.

> *Whatever games are played with us, we must play no games with ourselves.*
>
> — RALPH WALDO EMERSON

Marriage—spiritual union—is the symbol and sacrament of the fourth chakra. But the symbolic task we each face is to use our heart energy to recognize the divine qualities in each person who comes into our lives. And as with the energy of the third chakra, we first have to apply the energy to ourselves: we must love and respect ourselves before we can unite in spirit with others.

The fourth energy center is also the seat of compassion—for yourself and for others. Most people are more comfortable with second- and third-chakra expressions of self-appreciation than with love for themselves. Rewarding yourself with a dessert or some other treat after a bad day, for example, is acceptable self-care. But to love your self and to have a commitment to honor and respect who you are and what your purpose is remains an enormous hurdle, because many people are afraid that this smacks of narcissism. But just as you make a vow to honor a partner in marriage, you must make personal vows that serve as your emotional and spiritual guideposts. For instance, you might agree in some cosmic way to live "at the ready" for certain situations that arise, and vow that, "I could never leave a crying child," or, "I could never forgive myself if I didn't help a friend." These are not just highly emotional declarations, but vows that are heard and recorded, and tell the universe to use you to fulfill them. Personal vows acknowledge that you are conscious of what is critical to your emotional well-being and spiritual purpose.

Vows of the heart, like marriage vows, keep your heart permanently attuned to that commitment. It takes courage to do that. A heart-based commitment, in which an individual agrees in some cosmic way to live at the ready should a situation arise that matches his or her commitment, would include "I could never leave a crying child" or "I would never forgive myself if . . ." These are not just highly emotional declarations. They are vows that the universe hears and records; and they tell the universe to use us to fulfill them.

The following letter is an enchanting example of the power of a heart vow. Artemis E. writes, "A long time ago I took a personal growth course that had thirty people. They voted me a 'taker,' meaning someone who always looks after his own interests first, never sharing with others, a me-me-me person. I vowed from then on to be a giver. Later I was working on the issue of creating abundance and had to keep a record of things I was grateful for. I really decided I wanted to share my abundance with others. Initially I extended that to friends and family and now to all people. Abundance means more than money; it means sharing my talents, knowledge, kindness, and love. People are always astounded by surprise acts of kindness. The other day I was shopping and saw a real royal pair of gloves in this fancy shop. I had to have these gloves but when I got to the rack, I noticed that two poorly dressed women were admiring the gloves. I asked if they were going to buy them and they told me they were just visiting their friend who worked in the store. Once they moved to the front of the store, I bought them each a pair of these royal gloves. One of the women took my number off my credit card slip and called to say, 'Hello, madam, God loves you.' Funny that!"

Endless Love

God is love.

— I JOHN 4:8

Love is a form of grace. It gives us the stamina to endure what would normally be unendurable. Love's power is so great, we sometimes fear the demands it places on our lives. Love finds it difficult to say no. And abundant love can help improve even the worst of circumstances. Love transforms every action into a powerful instrument of change. The following story is a perfect illustration of the alchemical power of love and kindness. Jocelyn R. writes, "The most stunning acts of service provided to me have all come from my mother. It is almost impossible to choose just one of her gifts to me, but a fine example was when she drove with me from our farm in Saskatchewan to Oberlin, Ohio, where I went to college. I had arranged to live with and care for Mary, a ninety-six-year-old retired classics professor, in return for room and board. Mary was all but blind and deaf and so strong-willed and outspoken that none of her friends or family had been able to clean her or her home for years. But she met her match with my mother who was as stubborn with gentleness as Mary was filled with 'piss and vinegar.' Mother and I began to dig out the house to make it livable while Mary complained that nothing had to be done. There were sixty-year-old preserves (dates on the labels) and maggots in the kitchen linens, and Mary smelled ripe from not bathing. Mother had nothing but compassion for Mary. As she scrubbed the dishes with bleach and gritty cleansers, Mother spoke gently with Mary and by the time my mother left, she had even managed to knit Mary a sweater. I could not have afforded to go to Oberlin College without this job with Mary and I could not have lived with Mary had my mother not come with to demonstrate such love."

If, for example, someone asked you, "How much money would it take for you to gain a sense that you are successful and have no more worries?" what would you say? Would you require hundreds, thousands, or millions of dollars to feel better? And how much do you think it would take to generate hope once again in someone's life? First, what is hope worth? Life without hope is hell, so hope is invaluable. Since hope is that precious, it should cost enormous amounts of money, yet it takes very little to bring hope into someone's life. Once hope is up and running life becomes worth living again.

People absolutely adore surprises—both giving them and receiving them. Again, it's not the size of the surprise that matters; it's the love that flows through the act that renews the spirit of everyone involved. That love lasts for a lifetime. Here's a great story about a group of people who knew how to provide a long-running invisible act of power. Writes Gary S., "When my friend was in his early twenties, he worked at a prep school in Manhattan teaching English, chairing the English Department, coaching basketball, and serving as the dean. For all these services, he was only paid enough money to support a third-floor walk-up railroad flat with the bathtub in the kitchen. He also had to support his two children who lived upstate with his ex-wife. As a result, he went into debt. Despite these hardships, however, he was and is a loving and generous son, grandson, brother, nephew, cousin, and friend. Everyone, except his multimillion-dollar employer, would offer to help ease his financial burden, but he cheerfully declined. Among those standing in line to become his benefactors were his parents and various family members, all of whom were repeatedly denied the honor. Since he always maintained his humor, poise, and grace under pressures of money, work, and parenting, I'm certain no one realized how stressful it was for him. Nevertheless, somebody knew and devised the perfect scheme to help him. One day, an envelope with his name on it, delivered by hand, appeared in his mailbox. In the envelope was a money order for three hundred dollars drawn from a neighborhood bank. When he interrogated those most likely to have executed this, they were convincingly surprised and refused to take any credit. They continued to disavow any knowledge of the money order that continued to appear monthly for almost two years.

"He had no choice but to cash the checks and spend what came to be called the 'mystery money.' However, true to form, he would perform a ritual on the way home from cashing the money orders, giving some of the money to a homeless or needy person. I was with him on one such walk home when we saw five boys, no more than ten years old, attempting to sneak into the movies by climbing a fire escape in the back of the theater. Minutes later, they had tickets in hand, purchased by the mystery money. I learned that giving is the most pure when it is done for its own sake."

Love and Healing

Thou shall love thy neighbor as thyself.

—LEV. 19:18

At the end of the day, how we have treated each other on our life journeys is all that matters. All words and acts of kindness are vessels of healing. But when love is involved, their power becomes even greater. So do the demands on those who offer to serve. The love that motivates a person to volunteer his or her time to a charitable event is not the same as the love that devotes days and months to care for another individual. Again, let me emphasize that one type of love is not better than another; both are absolutely necessary to human life. But we grow and evolve to become able to manage greater commitments. We love our families and friends; we learn to love our neighbors, community, and fellow citizens, and to have compassion for all of humanity. The depth to which we allow ourselves to sense the needs of another person, to intuit his or her emotional pain and fear, and to help him or her, reflects the maturity of our spirit.

Love is all we have, the only way that each can help the other.

—EURIPIDES

In the following story, Hannah H. shares her awakening and capacity to provide love to another and the awesome power of healing that resulted. "My own severe illness taught me how important it is to have a few people to carry your life while you concentrate on getting well. In 1981, I was very ill and had been diagnosed with a 'terminal' illness. It took me more than two years to recover. In 2001, as I was preparing to move, sell my home, my business, and rearrange my life, a man I had partnered with for volunteer community mediation was diagnosed with cancer. He was trying to manage by himself, being brave and independent. When I learned of his health challenge, I made his recovery a priority in my life. John moved in with our family. We fed him whatever he could eat during his throat surgery and radiation treatments, drove him to the hospital daily for chemo and radiation, supported him through his surgery, and lined up volunteers to care for him. His financial world began to crash during his illness. Together with two other friends and his permission, we went to his home, tore off the back porch, which was falling apart, cleaned out twenty years of accumulated trash, sorted through his financial papers, and discovered five years' worth of unpaid bills. We hired an advocate to resolve his tax situation and handle his medical bills. We held a garage sale to raise cash. We resolved the notices from the city regarding his property, painted his house, found volunteers to reroof his place and also to fix the leaks. We paid for his daughter to come from California to be with him for a while and completed all the repairs on his house. Happily, John survived the cancer and returned to a new home and a functional life. He continues to serve the community as a volunteer peacemaker and mediator."

Such is the power of love. Without a doubt, this devotion helped John heal. We can never really measure or feel the full effect of our love upon another. No one can ever know the way in which love seeps into our minds and hearts to reorder our thoughts and fight off waves of self-pity or depression. But love opens wide the portal of grace. Like the power of prayer, love can build walls against despair and give us the courage to survive the greatest challenge.

If I speak in the tongues of men and of angels, but have not love, I am only a resounding gong or a clanging cymbal. If I have the gift of prophecy and can fathom all mysteries and all knowledge, and if I have a faith that can move mountains, but have not love, I am nothing. If I give all I possess to the poor and surrender my body to the flames, but have not love, I gain nothing.

— 1 COR. 13

Martin Buber tells this affecting story in his book *Tales of the Hasidim:*

HOW THE RABBI OF SASOV LEARNED HOW TO LOVE
Rabbi Moshe Leib told this story:

How to love men is something I learned from a peasant. He was sitting in an inn along with other peasants, drinking. For a long time, he was as silent as all the rest, but when he was moved by the wine, he asked one of the men seated beside him, "Tell me, do you love me or don't you love me?" The other replied, "I love you very much." But the first peasant replied, "You say that you love me, but you do not know what I need. If you really loved me, you would know." The other had not a word to say to this and the peasant who had put the question fell silent again.

But I understood. To know the needs of men and to bear the burden of their sorrow—that is the true love of men."

Often love has to be tough in order to help or protect someone. And tough love takes courage. It is much easier to walk away from a problem than to take a deep breath and confront someone. Confrontations make us so nervous that we tend to use anger rather than loving compassion because anger buffers our vulnerabilities. But love can help you through a difficult but necessary act of service, as is illustrated beautifully in the following couple of letters.

Writes Lisa M., "Some years ago I was going through a dark night of the soul. I was so confused and frustrated. I had always relied on my intellect to guide, collect, analyze, predict, control . . . but intellect does not work in the dark night. Most terrifying for me, I was seemingly without purpose. After some months, presumably when I was ready, the act of service which turned me around was when my loving husband said, with caring and a deep sense of resignation (as I complained about something not making me happy), 'I'm beginning to think you'll never be happy again.' He didn't complain. He stated a fact. And it pulled me out of myself for long enough to see what effect I was having on those who loved me, and also to give myself a reality check: it made me envision a future where, however it occurred, this phrase *would* pass. I would be happy again."

Writes Lynne L., "I'm quite lucky to have a friend who can go beyond initial feelings to really see where I'm coming from. We've been friends since the late sixties. There are times in life when my nose has gotten out of joint, paranoia has crept in, and I've mistakenly thought my friend's motives were other than they were. And I'd accuse her. Her service to me was in being able to see me so clearly that she knew it wasn't her at all. And her magical and miraculous response was to work with me from the perspective of how can I help my friend come back into alignment with the truth and love we share for each other."

Healing does not require that we deeply or intimately love another person. Acts of respect are also powerful conduits for healing energy, whether we hold open a door or share prayer space. As I organized these letters, I noted that numerous people listed "small but thoughtful" social habits they practice because civility makes for a better life environment in general. The habit mentioned most often by far was being conscious of holding a door open for someone. Let's put a symbolic perspective on the significance of holding a door open for someone. To 'have a door slammed in your face' is a universally recognized act of rejection, and is especially painful when it is done on purpose. People have told me painful stories about their families, saying, "They slammed the door closed in my face." Symbolically, holding open a door represents acknowledgment and respect for the other person. It is a visible act with invisible power, as is a phone call from a friend just when you need it most.

Miranda L. recalls: "The night before my divorce was final I was doing the 'What if I end up regretting this?' dance. I knew it was just fear talking and not my heart but I couldn't seem to stop it. Then the phone rang. It was my friend Becky, whose face had come to me the week before in meditation. I'd been guided to ask her to pray for me, but being a little shy about asking directly, I asked her husband to relay the message. When she phoned, I assumed he had told her about my request. I was wrong. Becky's husband had forgotten the message completely. She was calling about something else. I then told her what was happening for me and how I had been guided to ask for her prayers. She then told me that she had been divorced before as well, so she knew what I was going through. And then she did the most extraordinary thing—something I would never have thought to ask for. Instead of just reciting the usual platitudes people resort do in times like these, such as, 'You know it's all going to be fine in the end' and 'It's hard now, but the pain will pass,' Becky did something different. She acted as a mirror, reflecting to me who she knew me to be. She didn't mention my husband or the divorce or the pain I was feeling. Basically, she told me that I had been an inspiration to her because I was so clear in following my spiritual path. In helping me see and focus on who I was rather than on what I was feeling, she allowed me to realize that I did indeed have all the clarity I needed. My anxiety vanished in that phone call. She was an angel. Without her gift, I would never have been open to seeing all the signs of support around me."

A Little Love Goes a Long Way

The opposite of love is not hate, it's indifference.

— ELIE WIESEL

The following letters portray different faces of love's healing energy. The first letter is one of tender, conscious intention that comes straight from the heart. The author is Japanese and her story has not been edited to read in perfect English, as her words communicate the beauty of her message. Writes Takako I.: "I have impartial mind and always try to think others nice people. In Japan, people hardly give unknown others smiles in public, but after I learned it's a very good custom you have in the United States, I have always smiles or happy feelings to others. Sometimes when I had a trouble in the train or in the street, someone helped me and I felt my heart full of gratitude. And this made me feel that unknown, smileless people may have warm feelings and this idea encouraged me a lot."

Similarly, Bonnie E. writes: "I am always helping others whenever I see someone who needs it. An old school friend whose husband had just died looked so sad and lost standing in the check-out line at the supermarket. I didn't even think, I just walked up to her and said, 'Hi, how are you? I just heard about your husband.' I gave her a hug because she really seemed to need one and told her she could call me if she ever wanted to. She never called but told my husband later how much it had meant to her."

Fourth-chakra intuition is just like Bonnie described; you don't think about something, you act and then realize you acted without conscious thought. Often we hesitate when these impulses arise because of the fear that our intentions or efforts might get rejected. My experience with these impulses is that they are fully appreciated by their recipients. Intuitive impulses move faster through our natures than logical thought. The following letter is a lovely example of a fourth-chakra impulse that proved a healing blessing to both the giver and the receiver. Writes Joanne A., "Last week I was at my oncologist's office and the receptionist had commented to me how beautiful she thought my earrings were. Without hesitation I took them off and gave them to her because I knew deep in my heart that she would like to have them and that they would make her happy.

Two days later I received a thank-you note from her telling me that not only did I warm her heart with the earrings, but that was the first act of unselfish kindness anyone had done for her since her husband of thirty years passed away a few weeks earlier. I was floored."

When your own heart is in an emotional crisis, the universe may send guidance through a trusted friend because you are too unfocused to perceive clearly for yourself. Writes Pamela C.: "Still numb from my husband's affair and new child, I quickly found the beautiful gift of friends. Their gifts and hearts and healing talents made a huge difference. I was surprised, however, by the friends who showed up in my hometown. One friend came to the door, gave me a hug, rolled up her sleeves, and spent two full days helping me pick out colors of paint to give my house a new look. She brought a couple of beautiful pictures to go with the new look as well. She then volunteered to gather friends to make a quilt. I was not interested in any quilting at this time, but the quilt would come to represent this time and the value and the gift of love of my friends. It remains a cherished representation of this learning."

Courage takes many forms and manifests differently in each of the chakras; there is intellectual courage (sixth chakra), physical courage (third), and creative courage (second). In many cases, it takes pure guts to respond to fourth-chakra impulses, as illustrated in this letter from Rhonda L. which shows how intuition will push through fears and hesitation: "Around eight years ago, my brother was arrested and sent to jail. In our city, everyone awaiting trial is placed in a remand prison that has to be maximum security to cover those who have been charged with the more serious crimes. It was very traumatic for my brother and our family. I asked lots of questions and discovered more about the booking process, the hours, the forms that had to be filled in, ID requirements, restrictions on what each visitor could take in, and clothing regulations. Workplace health and safety regulations required that 'closed-in' shoes be worn by all visitors—no sandals or any type of open-toe shoes were allowed. Anyone not complying with regulations would not be allowed to visit.

"While waiting to see my brother I saw a number of people wearing sandals. Obviously they didn't know the rules and when their name was called, they didn't pass inspection and weren't allowed to visit. Some of these people had traveled long distances by public transportation and were devastated that after waiting so long, they would have to wait another week. The following week, I noticed a young woman who looked very stressed because she was wearing sandals. I felt so awful for her and then suddenly realized that I had a spare pair of shoes in the car. I asked her if she would like my spare pair of shoes and she gratefully accepted. Each week after that I brought a bag of shoes with me, which I gave to anyone who needed them for their visit. Most people who visit prisoners have faces that show lives full of pain and darkness. For a short time I was able to add a bit of lightness to some of those faces."

> *Joy and sorrow are inseparable . . . together they come and when one sits alone with you . . . remember that the other is asleep upon your bed.*
>
> —KAHLIL GIBRAN

Grief is a pain so great that it is almost a physical presence inside you. We need at times to learn to bear it alone, even when we have a willing entourage of friends and family to help us heal. The death of a spouse or child can cause waves of discomfort in a grieving person's social circle. Death engenders many superstitions and other parents and married couples unconsciously fear the trauma is contagious and may follow them home. This is one of the reasons that people say, "Call me if there is anything I can do for you" instead of saying, "I'll call you to check in regularly while you go through this." The bereaved person rarely picks up the phone to call for emotional support because asking for help is wretchedly difficult, particularly when one is emotionally distraught. At the end of these many letters that people have written to me, they note, "I am usually the one offering to help but I am very uncomfortable having to ask." This social fact of life makes the following story extraordinary.

Writes Brenda L.: For many years my husband and I had tried to conceive a child. After enduring many months of treatments and failures at the fertility clinic, we were advised that any more treatments would compromise my health and that maybe it was time to let it go. I was crushed. This was not the future I had envisioned. I had always dreamed of having children. It took awhile but I grieved and eventually came to terms with it. This no sooner happened when I found myself pregnant. I had gone to the doctor concerned that my cycle hadn't fully started and I was wondering if all the drugs had taken a toll on me. As I sat in the examining room, I prepared to hear the worst, only what I heard was, "Brenda, you're pregnant.' I didn't believe her. I made the doctor say it again, 'Brenda, you're pregnant.' Then I had her tell my husband. The look on his face was priceless. A part of me was flying, not listening to the doctor and my husband talk about the spotting. I remember hearing the words, 'high risk' and 'we'll have to monitor her process closely.' What were they talking about? Nothing could happen. Everything in the world was perfect. I shared my news with family and friends. I have wonderful women friends that had been by my side through my whole fertility ordeal. When we got together, I shared my news and we cried and laughed with happiness; after all, they were now becoming honorary aunts.

"A week or so passed. Then one morning, I awoke in extreme pain unable to move. My husband called an ambulance and I was rushed to the emergency room. After an ultrasound it was determined that my pregnancy was ectopic and my baby was dying. Without surgery I would die also. I begged the doctor to find any other way to save my baby but was told that surgery was the only option. I awoke from surgery sore and numb. I had nothing inside of me. No baby. No fallopian tube. No hope at all for children. No tears. Nothing. It was a comforting place, actually. Nothing could hurt me because nothing could get in. I lay in my hospital bed looking at the wall, holding my husband's hand.

"Then my dearest friend, Laura, came to visit. She sat at a chair by my bed, held my hand, and cried. She never said a word. She just cried. I looked at her in disbelief. Why was she crying? I patted her hand and told her, 'Shhhh. It's okay. Everything will be all right.' Still not saying a word, she continued crying. She then stood up and told me she loved me, kissed my cheek, and left. I was dumbfounded. What was that all about? My husband had left to give us privacy and when he returned, he asked what we talked about. I told him 'nothing' and went to sleep.

"It wasn't until several weeks later that I realized that Laura was the wisest woman I know. During those first few days of shock and despair, when I couldn't cry, she cried *for* me. She had held that space while I endured the numbness and pain of losing a child. When I did cry, I knew I had the support of a friend. No judgment, no expectations. Just there for me. I believe now that an act of service is something done out of love for another without any expectation of payment in any form. Laura didn't expect anything from me. She came to cry for her friend. I will always love her."

Connie C. wrote of her lovely practice, "I am inclined to acts of service associated with people (friends or strangers) who have lost a loved one, whether through death or divorce. I don't write notes or call, saying, 'I don't know what to say.' I know what to say and I say it. What comes is often driven by Spirit. After the initial contact, I follow up, often repeatedly, to find out how the person is doing. I also do this with people who have been ill and/or hospitalized."

And I have to include this touching story from Nancy K., who wrote, "I was in a state of deep grief and crying all day and night. A friend of mine came over one day with two shopping bags filled with boxes of tissues—all kinds, colors, scented, and unscented. We put them everywhere, all over my apartment. It made me laugh for the first time in weeks. And it was exactly what I needed—I used up every box. Her gesture told me that she understood my need to cry and she was offering the only comfort she could think of. It was a gift I will never forget."

The Healing Authority of Forgiveness

The best deed of a great man is to forgive and forget.

—QUR'AN 64:14

If you are offering your gift at the altar, and there remember that your brother has something against you, leave your gift there before the altar and go; first be reconciled to your brother and then come and offer your gift.

—MATT. 5:23–24

Although love is the key energy of the fourth chakra, forgiveness is the command. Few of the letters I received spoke of forgiveness as an act of service, yet nothing is more powerful than a single act of forgiveness. Consider how Jesus devoted his entire life to teaching forgiveness. His last act on the cross was to forgive those who persecuted him and ask God to forgive others: "Forgive them, Father, for they know not what they do."

To be unable to forgive is to live in hell, burdened, miserable, angry. Our egos hope those at whom we are angry are living in anticipation that we will one day forgive them. But most likely the person for whom you hold a grudge could not care less about your misery. He has moved on and you are stuck. Forgiveness is a powerful act that is healing to you. After all, the person you resent does not have to live in your body; you do.

Take back your spirit from the past. Get in present time and forgive the people who have hurt you. A ritual prayer in some churches asks for the divine grace to be forgiven and to forgive others. "Our father, who art in heaven . . . Forgive us our trespasses [sins] as we forgive those who trespass [sin] against us." Notice the feeling in your heart as you invite divine grace in and the softening that occurs in any block of anger or pain that has frozen in time. You have doubtless made missteps for which divine grace will forgive you.

If you asked your heart, "What is the greatest service I need to do in order to heal and to feel at peace?" what would you intuit as the response? The most frequent response I get to this question when I ask it at my seminars is: "My heart is telling me to be of service to others and that, through service, I will earn the interior tranquillity and the meaning in life that I am seeking."

The second most frequent response is, "I'm not sure." Now, anytime a person says, "I'm not sure," what he is really saying is that he doesn't like what his intuition just told him. Usually he's been told to forgive something that still burdens the heart.

Mary Jane A. writes of forgiveness: "I feel I missed an opportunity a few years ago when my aunt was dying. It came to me one day that I needed to tell my dad that he only had a short time left to ask my aunt for her forgiveness. I think I felt a combination of fear and anger toward him—fear that he might react angrily toward me and anger about the injustices that I knew of in the way he had treated her. Why didn't I just get over this and tell him? I have no idea why I hesitated. Shortly before my aunt died, these profound words came to me as a message from her soul to mine, 'Why have we allowed fear to keep us from each other's hearts?' "

Sue B. writes: "My father-in-law recently passed away, but before he did, I witnessed a wonderful and inspiring time of a family coming together for a final farewell to a loved one. Two days before he died, he finally said, 'I love you' to all his family. He had never spoken these words before in his life. In that moment, I looked at everyone at his bedside and immediately knew that all was forgiven from the past. Everyone's face reflected this. This was an act of service carried out by a man barely conscious, but we became aware that he was very conscious of what he had said in that moment to all who stood by his bed. This only confirmed for me that the body is indeed weak but the spirit lives on."

Charlene T. observed: "When I was going through a time of great difficulty, my dear friend Grace shared a great truth with me. Everything comes from love, even when it doesn't feel that way. Chris Griscom says that even those who do those things to us which bring us suffering are performing a great service, for we are being given information through that experience about where we need to bring light." I wholeheartedly agree with this teaching and absolutely adore the fact that "Grace" gave her friend this message.

The final story for this chapter is about healing and an enchanting divine intervention. Writes Sally S.: "My partner was on a ski holiday in France but I discovered he was not with the group of guys he had said he was with, but with a rather troubled lady who had come into our lives. She was hugely manipulative and had an ulterior motive with my boyfriend. I discovered my partner's and this lady's whereabouts through her husband. As I pieced together events leading up to this one, I found myself drinking to numb my pain. At that point, I had been drinking to excess for some time in my life. I had sought outside help and had asked my partner to help me by not stocking the house with alcohol. He didn't help; the place was like a pub and it seemed to be further encouraged by this lady who sent over case loads of wine.

"This lady worked in a bank. Having drunk much of the wine and now on my own in the house thinking about my partner and this woman trying to murder me with alcohol, I decided to phone her bank branch. It was around 10 P.M. I do not know who I thought would answer the phone at that hour, but someone did. A man answered and I was so surprised that I asked, 'Who is this?' 'The bank robber,' came the reply in the most beautiful and memorable Liverpudlian accent. I laughed and fell for the voice instantly.

" 'You sound just like John Lennon,' " I said. 'What on earth are you doing in the bank at this time of night?' J. L., as I called him, kept up descriptions all night as to how he was wiring the safe and using explosives. I roared with laughter. We kept up the phone calls back and forth to each other all night. I was never so happy and having such fun at the most miserable time of my life. We spent until 6 A.M. swapping life stories, laughing until the tears rolled. Then he sent me a fax with the message, 'Hang in there, sweetheart. You can beat the world.' "

"He checked in on me at 8 A.M. to see if I was okay. And then he checked in a few months later and then a year later and we marveled at the changes and growth in our lives and the importance of love. His name is Jim and I found out from the guard at the bank that he was an electrician who had been hired to put in an alarm system that evening. I was so blessed that this man appeared in my life when he did."

Symbolically, Sally's emotional alarm was going off and a compassionate electrician was able to help her rewire her currents to survive.

Love is patient, love is kind. It does not envy, it does not boast, it is not proud. It is not rude, it is not self-seeking, it is not easily angered, it keeps no record of wrongs. Love does not delight in evil but rejoices with the truth. It always protects, always trusts, always hopes, always perseveres.

— 1 COR. 13

Examining the Heart of Your Fourth Chakra

There is no such thing as an insignificant act of love. The power of love exists in every breath we take. Our intention transforms energy into a healing power that infuses our thoughts and deeds, from holding a door open for someone to staying up all night with someone who has lost a child.

The following examination of your fourth-chakra intuition asks how willing you are to open yourself to others.

<u>As the Giver:</u>
1. To what type of person or situation does your fourth chakra connect?
2. When have you acted on fourth-chakra impulses? Were you pleased or disappointed by the outcome?
3. What scares you most about opening to your fourth-chakra intuition?

4. Are you aware when you close your heart to someone?
   What motivates that response?
5. What are the parameters that your heart has set to limit
   what you will allow yourself to give?

As the Receiver:
1. Are you presently in need of emotional support?
2. Is it difficult for you to receive love and support from
   others?
3. Are you in need of forgiveness or do you need to forgive
   another?

A FOURTH-CHAKRA PRAYER

I open my heart to receive love. I may not feel this love enter immediately, but I shall live in trust that love begins to flow into me the moment I request it and that this flow is endless. I turn my attention to my heart intuition and I open myself to receiving one clear insight. I bless those who surround me and support me and those whose support I benefit from whom I shall never meet in this lifetime.

And here is a traditional Hebrew prayer:

You must love your G-d with all your heart, with every breath, with all you have. Take these words that I command you now to your heart. Teach them intently to your children, bind them as a sign upon your hand, and keep them visible before your eyes. Inscribe them on the doorposts of your house and on your gates.

CHAPTER 5

Gifts of Choice

To see what is right and not to do it is to lack courage or principle.
— CONFUCIUS

My first encounter with what I now think of as "fifth-chakra power" took place in less than a minute and changed my entire life. It happened when I was in my first year as an undergraduate at my Catholic college, where all freshmen had to take religion class. I had the attitude of, "Who needs to study that?" So I didn't, and I just assumed I would pass. By midsemester, I was on the road to a seriously failing grade. The professor, someone I hold in deep esteem to this day, stopped me in the hall outside her class to say, "You're not doing well in my class. You obviously have a good mind, and it is unfortunate that no one has yet taught you how to utilize the mind effectively." And then she walked away . . . just like that.

I was stunned by this exchange. I had just been told something that ordinarily would have humiliated me, but I felt inspired—empowered. I could not get over it. Everything about that moment impressed itself on me, most especially my professor's detached style of delivery. She was able to tell me something I very much needed to hear without making me feel like a failure. Her lack of a private agenda allowed me to absorb only the grace and wisdom of her guidance. In that exchange, I learned about the power of choice and intention. I remembered how this professor had introduced herself on the first day of class, stating, "My intention is to teach you to the best of my ability. Whether you like me or not is of no consequence to me. My job is to teach." I had never heard anyone before in my life state that it didn't matter whether she was liked or not. At the time, I, like most young women, thought that being liked and appreciated was the goal of everything we did. My professor opened the domain of the transpersonal to me. The purity of intention that she so beautifully exhibited was one of her most wonderful lessons.

The Consciousness of Your Fifth Chakra

Our deepest fear is not that we are inadequate. Our deepest fear is that we are powerful beyond measure. It is our light, not our darkness, that most frightens us.

— MARIANNE WILLIAMSON

The Sanskrit name for the fifth chakra means "purified" and refers to the spiritual path of becoming conscious of why we do what we do—our intention. As we increase in awareness, we take responsibility for the consequences of our actions. This level of power also requires the practice of right speech, as Buddhists call it, for the fifth chakra is at throat level. Right speech involves the weighing of every thought and word, speaking honestly but with good judgment, since everything we say affects the people around us. At this fifth level of power, we are meant to act toward others in ways that transmit a great strength of spirit and conviction. With every choice, we are meant to "Surrender Personal Will to Divine Will"—the motto of this energy center.

When the Buddha taught right speech to his son, he first asked him to reflect on what he would say and make sure that his "verbal action" would not be hurtful to others. If it would be hurtful, give it up; if it would increase happiness and create happy results, then pursue it. If it unexpectedly causes hurt, reflect on it and "confess it" to yourself and even a teacher or a mentor or knowledgeable friend.

It takes courage to be honest with ourselves, too. Often we don't want to face our real reasons for doing things and face up to any negative consequences of our actions. There are many kinds of courage that influence the choices we make. For example, we need great physical courage to jump into a burning building to rescue a child or push someone out of the path of a speeding car. Yet it can take a different kind of emotional courage to speak up and stand up against an injustice or to intervene in someone's personal life. One man told me, "I would much rather save someone from fire or drowning than to have to tell a close friend that I know he is an addict. I know this because I have rushed into a fire to save someone and I do have a friend who is an addict, and I have yet to find the courage to save him."

The fifth chakra, then, represents acts of service that require a more conscious quality of personal courage. At this level, you face your intuitive revelations, accept them, *and* act on them. You make tough life choices for yourself and when you extend yourself to others.

I see the Christian sacrament of confession as a symbol of fifth-chakra power because confession—to ourselves in our thoughts or to a clergy member—involves absolute honesty and the courage to admit our wrongdoing. It also represents purification, because you are consciously withdrawing energy from actions you regret having set in motion. As Maya Angelou has written, "History, despite its wrenching pain, cannot be unlived, but if faced with courage, need not be lived again." We face the facts and face the many sides of ourselves at the fifth level of power. And we surrender our personal will to divine will.

The believer who participates in human life, exposing himself to its torments and suffering, is worth more than the one who distances himself from its suffering.

—HADITH OF IBN MAJAH

There's a traditional story told of a wise old man who could answer seemingly every question posed to him and two boys who wanted to try to trick him. The two boys decided to catch a bird and take it to the old man and ask him, "This bird that we're holding: is it alive or dead?" If the old man said it was alive, they would crush it to prove him wrong; if he said it was dead, they'd turn it loose and let it fly away. So they trapped a bird, took it to the old man, and asked him, "Is this bird that we're holding alive or dead?" And the wise man looked at them and said, "Really, it is in your hands."

The fifth chakra is the seat of your power of choice and intention—your will. From a metaphysical perspective, making a choice converts energy into matter, thought into form. You conduct this alchemical ritual thousands and thousands of times a day, from your choice of dress to your decision to help a stranger or mentor a colleague. Learning to manage this power of choice is synonymous with the right action that the Buddha taught.

Eventually, through exercising your power of choice judiciously, you learn to see how you and your actions can work in harmony with the world around you. You may experience the grace of living in harmony with the universe only a handful of times, but the experience is characterized by a feeling of trust and a rapport with your surroundings.

Some of the letters I received reported lifesaving harmonious experiences; some writers heard instructions, such as "Slow down, now," when they were driving, to which they reacted and avoided serious accidents. They did not have time to question or evaluate the guidance; they simply followed it, a typical response to a divine intervention. Others were directed to speak to strangers and give them information that "just came through" to them. And others received inner guidance about themselves.

Suzanne O. writes, "I hesitated to help myself ten years ago when I was going through a depression. Had I stopped and listened to that inner voice that was screaming at me, I could have saved myself ten years of suffering."

We make choices based upon available data. "If I eat this, then . . . ; if I wear this, then . . . ; if I say this, then . . ." We have visible, physical, and invisible, energetic data. Energetic data asks us to respond to it in creative, potentially transformative responses. For example, a person I know had to have surgery to remove a cancerous tumor. For years prior to finding the tumor, she had been having numerous energetic—intuitive—signals, "funny feelings" that something was wrong and that she was "just not herself." She continually blamed her increasingly negative emotional and physical health on her marriage and job; translation—she clearly identified two stress factors but decided not to do anything about them. Her response was, "What can I do? He won't change and I need the job." Her emotional and psychic stress increased as the years passed, manifesting, as repressed intuitive stress often does, in temper tantrums and blaming other people's shortcomings for her anxiety. Finally, the energetic stress broke through to the physical as breast cancer. Once the illness became physical, her choices were limited: she had to respond to the physical disease. Had she listened to her intuition's warnings about the dire need to change her life to get and be healthy, however, she could have alleviated the awful emotional stress she was under and possibly—possibly—even prevented a physical health crisis.

It is risky to draw a direct line from stress to illness, and through the years, I have learned that there is no such thing as a single emotional, physical, or environmental factor on which to blame an illness. Still, sometimes it is obvious that bad health habits, like smoking, or constant stress do make us sick. We have to learn to take care of ourselves, listen to and decipher our bodies' signals, and keep ourselves out of the path of illness. As you grow in conscious awareness at this fifth-chakra level, your inner world gains authority over the physical world, and you can hear and act on interior promptings more clearly.

A letter from Sheri H. illustrates the courage it can take to act on your intuition: "A few years ago I was a volunteer at a local hospital. I found out a baby had been brought into the emergency room not breathing. Immediately I thought SIDS since in 1988 my fourth child died of it at three months old. I left the office I was working to see if I could offer support to the parents. The mother was outside with her father-in-law, wailing, 'She was fine when I put her down. How can she be dead?' Listening to her cry, I waited until the time was right and slowly walked over to them. I excused my barging in at such a time, but offered her a piece of paper with my name and phone number, explaining that I'd lost a baby to SIDS and that if she needed help or support, she could call me. She reached out and hugged me and we both cried. We became good friends. That day I acted on my gut instinct to approach this grieving mother.

"The director of social services for the hospital saw this transpire and became so angry with me that she told the director of volunteers to fire me (even though I was a volunteer). She told me that I had no business interfering in people's grief because I was not trained in grief counseling. I asked her if she had even had a child die of SIDS. She told me no. I told her that I had and that made me an expert on the subject, adding that no amount of study could ever prepare one for what to do in such a situation like having to live through it does. The service I rendered that young mom stands out in my mind simply because I had to get outside myself and overcome my fear of meddling in other people's lives to find the courage to approach her."

I know I can do medical intuitive readings, but I also know I am not meant to do them for everyone. I consider myself "cosmically available"—that is my practice. I have a great deal of empathy for the numerous people who have been in that painful place of receiving direct guidance on which they lack the strength to take action. An intuitive who has not yet examined the meaning of personal courage will find himself in more than one painful crisis until he resolves any rational concerns of acting on nonrational guidance. In the letters I received, everyone shared a story about how much she regretted not having the courage to act on her intuitive guidance and the consequences of that choice. Everyone can relate to some circumstance in which, looking back, we wish we had had the courage then that it is hoped we have now.

> *Character cannot be developed in ease and quiet. Only through experience of trial and suffering can the soul be strengthened, vision cleared, ambition inspired, and success achieved.*
>
> —HELEN KELLER

Many of the letters I received reveal a fear of being perceptive and not knowing how to act or follow up on intuitive promptings. That fear has created a crisis of conscience for a number of people. Let me reassure you, we are not meant to act upon *all* intuitive hits, but we have yet to find a comfort zone that allows us to be comfortable *not* acting. I frequently sense a health imbalance in someone, but I rarely walk up to that person and say anything, nor do I feel I am supposed to say anything in all instances. If circumstances come together that support a discussion, I might then share my insights. But I use my judgment, as you must. There is no easy answer here. Countless people have told me that their intuitive abilities have created personal and social crises for them because they are not sure how to act on them. As a result, they end up at odds with their own abilities. We see this fear of intuition and choice portrayed even in our art and films.

The movie *Grand Canyon*, for instance, is peopled with everyday angels and synchronicities that bring together characters in ways that change their lives. One character finds an abandoned baby under a bush during her daily run when she impulsively alters her usual route. She believes she was meant to find and keep the baby, and argues with her doubting husband that, "Some kind of connection has been made and it has to be played out." Her husband, however, tries to end the discussion by saying his head hurts, but the woman says, "It's just an inappropriate response to get a headache in the presence of a miracle." It's inappropriate, yes, but when we fear instead of embrace the miracle, a headache is a pretty common response.

Some of the anxiety about how to act on intuition arises from our basic unwillingness to be open to guidance that pushes us past our usual limits, that makes us move outside our customary routine and circle. Most people only want to be intuitive enough to make wise life decisions for themselves. Once you are intuitively in motion, however, you stay in motion. You have to develop a secure sense of who you are and what tasks are yours to do in this life. Writes Julia C.: "When I was in high school, I watched many of the 'jock boys' tease an overweight and rather unattractive girl from the country. They would often make unflattering comments when they saw her or shout out a horrible nickname. I really felt bad for her, but I didn't have the courage to take on the jocks. After a while, she stopped coming to school. I forgot about her until my senior year. As part of my psychology class, we took a field trip to the state mental institution. As we were walking through the wards, we ran into this girl. She had lost a deal of weight and had become extremely attractive. Many of the same jocks who had tortured her were in this class trip. I watched her shrink from them and in that moment I wondered if she had been institutionalized as a result of how she had been treated in our high school. I wished with all my heart that I had had the courage to stand up for her and it made me wonder what would have happened if only one person had befriended her."

There is power in every word we say and every thought we think, but sometimes the greatest service we can offer is *not* to say something. Words are but one form of communication and they are not nearly as potent as the energy contained in our actions, including our thoughts, body language, eye contact, and facial expressions. You know that you trust the energy behind the words spoken to you far more than you do the words themselves. When you say something you don't mean, you know the other person picks that up. You can feel it.

We can also feel energetic support—both active and silent. In the course of organizing the letters, I was struck that no one mentioned a decision to withhold comments, criticism, or gossip from another person when it would be harmful or hurtful. This, too, can be an act of service. Ask yourself, "What possible motivation can there be to pass on hurtful, harmful information? Do you do that just for the sake of watching the cause and effect of a stream of negative information?" We can feel a rather wicked rush of power through negative words and gossip, and that rush is addictive. But in thoughtful, compassionate communications, lives are enhanced, healed, and changed forever, as illustrated by the following letter.

Writes Adam G., "I am a jazz musician and years ago was asked to put a jazz band together at the last minute for a posh ball at one of the British barracks in central London. None of the regular people I used were available, so on impulse I rang some very brilliant young jazz musicians who I knew vaguely through the music scene and who I thought may not be working on Saturday night. I had always wanted to play with these guys. I was surprised and flattered that they agreed to do the gig with me and I was nervous because I felt inferior. I remember losing my place in the music during a particularly wild piece of improvisation. The style that these musicians played was very far from the beat and was difficult to follow unless you were very experienced. One of them, who happened to be the one I admired the most, sensed that I was losing my place in the music. He picked up a cowbell and beat it in time like a metronome to help me hear where the pulse was. I was surprised and very delighted and it helped me play more freely. What he did helped me to feel included in the group and anchored rather than ashamed that I did not have the rhythmic sophistication that they had. We never spoke about it afterwards, but I felt extremely grateful and touched that he had actually helped a 'weaker' member of the group rather than becoming critical of me as is the case with many virtuoso musicians."

When one door closes another door opens; but we so often look so long and so regretfully upon the closed door, that we do not see the ones which open for us.

—ALEXANDER GRAHAM BELL

Many of the stories contained painful memories of discovering that the person about whom they had a gut feeling they should phone committed suicide or died of an illness. I know all too well

that feeling that invades my psyche and body when I don't want
to do something, but know I should, and I loathe that feeling . . .
it's like high anxiety blended with guilt and anger. Yet this feeling
is *meant* to be uncomfortable and evoke a response from us. It's
your survival intuition asking you to engage your heart, make a
choice, and do something.

This next letter is from a woman who received very strong
intuitive instructions, but chose not to respond. Note that it's
not the intuitive instructions that matter so much; it's her response and the reason why she made the decision she did that
haunts her.

Writes Connie M.: "A couple of years ago, I was hiking with
the Sierra Club in Dallas. It's extremely hot here in September
and it was a scorching day. Around a curve in the trail, we came
upon and man and a woman. The woman was on the ground
crying, holding a dead dog in her lap. Their dog had apparently
collapsed from heat exhaustion. Before I knew what was happening, I started to push my way toward the front of the group, toward the lifeless dog. I *knew* I could bring this dog back to life. All
I had to do was place my hands on him. I felt not myself and yet
truly myself. But in everyday life, I was not in touch with this
power, yet the part of me that was making its way toward the dog
accepted this power as an everyday occurrence. Then a voice in
my head said, 'Are you crazy? You can't help that dog.' And I
stopped in my tracks and stood there helpless like everyone else.
To this day, I think about that dog and I wonder what would have
happened if I had followed through."

Kara Z. writes of her own intuitive response to render an act
of service: "A few years back, I went to Guatemala to attend my
mother's funeral. While in a dry cleaners, I felt something funny
behind me, and saw a man trying to pull a woman from a car. I
turned around immediately and started walking toward the car
asking the man. 'What is it that you want?' He straightened out

and pointed a .45 at my forehead and I kept moving forward, with my arms straight down and the palms turned up, repeating the same question. He kept begging me to go back and I kept walking toward him. He threw the keys back at the woman and ran away. The incident had a lot of spectators and no one did a thing: they watched in silence. He had meant to kidnap her. I guess I stopped it."

Intuition and Courage

One should speak the truth and speak it pleasantly; one should not speak the truth in an unpleasant manner nor should one speak untruth because it is pleasing; this is the eternal law.

—LAWS OF MANU

We often hesitate to follow our intuitions out of fear. Most usually, we are afraid of the changes in our own life that our actions will bring. Intuitive guidance, however, is all about change. It is energetic data ripe with the potential to influence the rest of the world. To fear change but to crave intuitive clarity is like fearing the cold, dark night while pouring water on the fire that lights your cave. In the fifth chakra, the center of "choice and consequence," an insight the size of a mustard seed is powerful enough to bring down a mountain-sized illusion that may be holding our lives together. Truth strikes without mercy. We fear our intuitions because we fear the transformational power within our revelations.

When we fear to admit what we know, we get very skilled at being deliberately unconscious. Every parent who has ever poured months or years into denying his child's drug addiction knows this. Every wife who has ignored her husband's infidelities knows this. But ignoring the truth only creates more lies and destructive energy.

Once we admit a truth, however, our life is kicked into an orbit of change, whether or not we want it. Some of the letters tell of their writers' facing up to gut-wrenching feedback. They even appreciated the messenger, rather than shooting him. As a result of the writers' acceptance of the facts, positive personal change was able to take root in their lives.

Writes Sylvia L., "Acts of service don't always have to feel nice; the service comes when someone possesses the willingness to tell you something you need to hear when most likely you don't want to hear it. This is the kind of service that I get most often—a reality sandwich with truth. I often don't like to hear it, but bless those people in my life who overlook my personality and go straight to the deeper part of who I am. It makes me so mad, but it means the world to me. The truth is I am loved despite my forgetfulness."

Deb M. wrote, "When I was newly diagnosed with bipolar disorder, my rapid-cycling mood shifts and dependency scared away friends, relatives, neighbors, and, after a severe manic episode at work, my employer. I became housebound, depressed, suicidal, and was heavily drugged. My Avon lady began spending more and more time with me listening to my despair. She had hundreds of customers, worked day and night, but found extra time for me. She began taking me out to lunch during our bi-weekly visits. She shot down every excuse I had for not going—my unkempt appearance, no money, too tired. She got me out of my house, back into the sun, and walking (natural antidepressants). Now I hold open doors for others, listen to strangers. I recall when I was lonely and no one took the time to listen to me. I am giving back to others what most helped me—someone's caring attention. The only time I have ever doubted my openness was when I was raped by an acquaintance I trusted. Even then I knew that this openness is an essential part of me that I could not close up. This is my gift to the world—the ability to listen and empathize with all types of people."

Intuitive actions are not always about pain, however. On the sweet side of courageous sharing, Pat C. writes, "I made a resolution a year and a half ago to say aloud to the person I am speaking to any compliments or positive thoughts whenever they cross my mind. For years I had thought, 'Who cares about what I think?' When I realized that others cared less about *my* thinking about me and more about what I thought *about them* it became easier to share. What motivated me was seeing how people respond to compliments. Recently I started telling people what I was doing in the hope of spreading the habit."

Sometimes other people's traumas are meant to heal us from our own. Fifth-chakra power includes being receptive to other people's words and experiences, and grateful for the wisdom they are trying to impart. Healing can require a witness who can compassionately observe or listen to our grief and release it. A "healing witness" can be anyone from a therapist to a physician to a trusted friend or, as in the following letter, a compassionate stranger. When you are in the presence of a "healing witness," you must choose to accept the blessings of that moment.

Writes Janelle D., "To sit and listen while someone talks and allow that person to be with her feelings and experience her emotions without comment, and to create a safe space for that person to find her way through whatever passage she is making, is an act of service. I hitchhiked through Europe when I was twenty-one years old. I was raped and left in a remote area. When I regained enough composure, I tried to find a ride back to a populated area. I was picked up by three different men in three different vehicles. One was a truck driver who spoke neither of the two languages I spoke. He was concerned about what happened to me, but we could not communicate. The second man was an American who basically felt I got what I deserved. The third person to offer me a ride was an elderly man. He was dressed in a suit and had the sweetest smile. As soon as I got in the car, he noticed that I was upset and after a time asked me what was wrong, I told him and he was silent for a long time. Finally he took a deep breath and spoke. I wish I could remember his exact words because they were so eloquent. Essentially he said that he had been in a concentration camp during the war. Everyone in his family had died in the camps or had been killed because they were Jewish. He was the only one he knew who had survived the war. He had suffered so much and seen so much suffering that he knew God had a special purpose for keeping him alive. So now when he saw someone who seemed to need something, like me, he would try to help them because he knew what it was like to be alone, helpless, and without hope. And because he knew that, he could understand what these people felt and what they were going through. He said to me, 'You have had this terrible thing happen to you. God will give you the opportunity to help others because you have felt the pain that they have felt. God will guide you to do this as he has guided me all these years.' He then took me to the youth hostel, where I stayed the night, and he arranged for me to be able to stay during the day as well so that I could rest. I didn't have to do anything. The woman at the hostel took care of me because he asked her to. I never knew his name but because of him, I found comfort in his words and was able to rest and recover in a safe place."

This is healing grace in action.

The Courage to Make
Life-Changing Choices

You gain strength, courage and confidence by every experience in
which you really stop to look fear in the face. You are able to say to
yourself, "I have lived through this horror. I can take the next thing
that comes along." You must do the thing you think you cannot do.

— ELEANOR ROOSEVELT

The following letter represents a rare encounter with intuition, courage, and compassion. Writes Lorraine C., "When I was nineteen years old, a very large man got into my car and ordered me to drive to a certain place. I did not panic and after parking the car, I followed him into a house located behind a much bigger house. He talked with me for six hours. He was apparently newly released from the armed forces and played out a scenario of my being his girlfriend. When I felt it was okay for me to leave, I told him I had to get home. He walked me to my car, asking me to wear a dress and my hair down next time I visited. I drove away, knowing he had been so lonely that he had done this out of desperation. I also knew he was somehow at peace now."

Courage is not just about what you are willing to say to someone or admit to yourself. Courage is also required to admit when you have misjudged a person and then to go the distance to help that person emerge whole in this world. The following letter is an inspiring story of humility. Writes Barrie K., "When I was in tenth grade, my family moved from a suburban area with an excellent public school system into a city with mediocre public schools. My father had left us years before, my mother was on welfare and chronically depressed, and as the oldest of four, home life held no joy for me. We couldn't afford to live in the suburbs anymore, so we moved. When my mother took me to the principal's office at the new school to register, the principal complained that this school couldn't accommodate me academically. The two school systems were so different that my courses didn't match. And it was late in the school year. In my former school, I had been in all advanced-placement classes and done very well. School was the highlight of my life. The principal wanted to send me back to my old school, but my mother couldn't afford the bus fare. Finally I was put into a mixed bag of courses, one of which was advanced-placement biology. At my old school, it was a tenth-grade class, but at this new school, it was for seniors. Neither the teacher nor the students were pleased to see me arrive.

"About three days after I started school, we had an exam on genetics. The biology teacher said, 'You'll have to take it with the class.' I said I didn't mind because we had covered that topic in my old school. The exam was tough and I did as best I could. The teacher said he would have our grades the next day. When I arrived at class the next day, he asked me to step into his private office. He closed the door and stood over me with his arms crossed, saying, 'I don't know how you did it, being new at this school, but you are not leaving this room until you tell me how you got a copy of this exam and from whom.' I was in shock. No one had ever accused me of cheating before. He repeated with his voice raised, 'How did you get this exam?' I started to cry and he just stared at me. I said, 'Why do you think I cheated?' He replied, 'Because I made that exam impossible to finish in one hour. The questions just get harder. You not only got the answers right, you got farther in the test than anyone has in all the years I've given it. You could not do that without having the answers in advance.' I told him to call my teacher at my old school because we did all that material there. He said he would do just that and let me go.

"I heard nothing for about a week. The seniors were getting

ready to graduate. Finally that teacher asked me into his office. 'I've done some checking,' he said. 'You did know the material, apparently. After the seniors are gone, you and I will have a biology tutorial with special projects.' I was so relieved to have gained his approval. I really enjoyed the projects we did together in those two weeks. Perhaps more important was the attention from a considerate, male adult. Then he said, 'This high school is wasting your time. How would you like to finish high school a year early and then go right on to college?' And that is exactly what he arranged. I spent one more year finishing state requirements, bypassed my senior year, and went on to my freshman year in college. Furthermore, this teacher arranged for me to get a full four-year scholarship and work-study job for expenses. It was more than my parents could ever have provided for me. And he did it without recognition or reward of any kind.

"This teacher wanted me to go into medicine, but when I chose the humanities he didn't complain. I devoured higher education, went on to get a B.A., two M.A.'s, and a Ph.D., all in humanities. When I turned thirty, I became depressed because I knew I wasn't doing what I was supposed to do. One day in a bookstore, I read about now Dr. Albert Schweitzer had been a professor and then felt the calling to go into medicine. I thought that if he could do that, so could I. I added a D.O. to my list of degrees. As I graduated, I remember my biology teacher and sent him a letter so he would know that I had gone into medicine after all. And now I endeavor to use my hands to help the life and health of my patients."

Some of the best, high-voltage intuitive hits you receive tell you what you can do for others. Intuitive downloads on others' behalf are cosmic responsibilities, yet people often do shrug them off precisely because they are demanding. Let's face it, we have a "thing" about wanting to see the outcome before we agree to take action. We ask, "What's in it for me?" and "I just want to make sure I don't waste my energy or fail."

Let your deeds be done for the sake of heaven.

—MISHNAH, ABOT, 2:17

Writes Drew C., "A few years ago, a couple moved into our neighborhood which, at the time, was in fairly bad shape. The area had slowly started to go downhill and somehow the residents on the block just let it happen, including me. Well, this new couple set about fixing up their house immediately, painting the outside and grooming the landscaping. Little by little, their home began to look very charming. After they finished most of their repair work, they surprised all the rest of us by inviting us over for a barbecue. Warm and gracious, they, like the rest of us, did not have a great deal of money, but what they lacked in finances they certainly made up for in creativity. I wondered who the first would be of our group to compliment them on their home repairs and decorating. Finally, I did and that broke the ice. Soon a conversation started and they were very open and willing to share how inexpensive it was for them to fix this and repair that. By the end of the evening, they had volunteered to hold a small workshop on "how to renovate" our homes. Most of us on our block attended that first of many workshops, which turned out to be a wonderful social affair as we all brought food and desserts. Soon this became the social event of the month and from that emerged teams of working people who started with one house and then continued to repair all the rest of the homes on the block. Eventually our block became the talk of the town. During the holidays, we planned a decorating theme and together made the block look like a wonderland. The friendships and bonds that grew among us were incredible. Our block became a close, loving community. I have learned so much from this experience, not the least of which is all it took to set this incredible adventure in motion was to appreciate the talents of two good, generous people."

In a similarly wonderful story that celebrates the ability to act upon intuitive ideas that serve so many, Charles N. writes, 'Two years ago while on vacation in the Caribbean, I saw this small building that looked like a fort that I would have built in seventh grade. It turned out to be a school! I took pictures of all the cute kids and got the name of the teacher and the phone number. I thought maybe I could send them some books and pens when I got home. Later I thought, 'What good are a couple of pens and books going to do for these kids?' I have to admit I always wanted to be rich so I could help kids. Well, I was already forty-one years old and not rich, so I decided I didn't have to be rich to help out these kids. I decided to raise money for school.

"A friend of mine who was in the Caribbean offered her help and together we organized a raffle. We purchased two round-trip airline tickets to the Caribbean and a hotel donated three nights for the winners. A major rum distillery donated rum for a party. I worked very hard for months. I had to have raffle tickets printed up along with invitations to the event and I had to find a space in which to hold it. I blew up all the photographs of the children and hung them up on the walls of the venue. I am by nature a little lazy, but all this work was not work at all. It was fun and it made me feel so good. In the end we raised four thousand dollars and with that money, I bought supplies for three schools. The two schools received two computers and it made the news! It was the best experience of my life. A little effort can go a long way in a country not as abundant as ours. Now I sell my girlfriend's designer clothes to a secondhand store and the money, plus any extra money I can find, goes toward these three schools.

I am going back to the Caribbean this month to drop off two bags of supplies. I will go every year from now on."

Healing Insights of the Fifth Chakra

Is there a link between the quality of your health and the quality of your choices? Is there a consequence to your health when you repress intuitive insights? What happens within your body when you become "deliberately unconscious" as a way of sidestepping guidance? How involved is your biological health with your intuitive health? Although I have never read a medical article in which "repressed intuition" has ever been officially recognized as a source of stress, from my perspective the choice to ignore, avoid, or deny intuitive guidance is every bit as toxic as a bad habit. The involvement of your body with your intuitive nature exceeds the definition of the word *intimate*. Your body resonates to every intuitive hit you receive. Everyone has sensed that something is wrong at one time or another and has felt the high physical anxiety that comes with it. Similarly, when you recognize guidance but don't act on it out of fear, you can most certainly feel guilt, sadness, even depression. I would never link specific illnesses such as cancer or other life-threatening diseases to patterns of repressed intuitive behavior. And at the very least, you cannot be emotionally healthy while betraying your interior life.

Examining the Heart of Your Fifth Chakra

A wise decision will always feel congruent to your mind and spirit. This is true whether you are wondering how to help a friend or trying to decide whether to follow through on a hunch. Following intuitive wisdom will never leave you with a sense of betrayal or a feeling that you have been shattered, regardless of how demanding a commitment might become.

There is no more powerful act than that of making a choice. Choose to seek the symbolic or spiritual presence in every moment and situation of your life. Even the smallest positive action can help someone heal.

The examination of your fifth chakra takes you into the center of your intuition and decision-making processes:

As the Giver:
1. How do you identify the difference between mental feedback and intuitive instructions?
2. Have you ever been afraid of your intuitive guidance?
3. Have you ever had the experience of reading another person even though you did not want to?
4. Under what conditions are you likely to become "deliberately unconscious" when you are around another person's problems?
5. Are you especially intuitively clear when you are needed?

As the Receiver:
1. Is there a choice you need to make at this time in your life that you fear?

2. Do you feel that your life is dependent more on the choices other people make than on your own?

3. Do you feel that your interior life is at a breakthrough point, but you fear moving more deeply into spiritual space?

A FIFTH-CHAKRA PRAYER

Grant that I have the courage to receive intuitive instructions and guidance without fear. In this moment, I consciously embrace guidance for my next step in helping myself with _____ and in helping another person to _____. I acknowledge that guidance is delivered to me instantly; I need only to feel its presence and to listen.

And here is a traditional Hebrew prayer:

Dear G-d, protect my tongue from evil, and my lips from telling lies. May I turn away from evil and do what is right in your sight. Let me be counted among those who seek peace. May my words of prayer and my heart's meditation be seen favorably, Beloved One, my rock and my redeemer. May the one who creates harmony above make peace for us and for all who dwell on Earth. And say: Amen.

CHAPTER 6

Gifts of Wisdom

Knowledge can be communicated, but not wisdom. One can find it, live it, be fortified by it, do wonders through it, but one cannot communicate and teach it.

— Hermann Hesse, *SIDDHARTHA*

Sometimes we are blessed to meet a person whose wisdom is so absolute that it recalibrates our entire scale of values. I was blessed to meet such a person in Jack, a magical man who had simply made the choice to appreciate every day of his life, no matter what it held in store for him. Many other people have tried to do this, with varying degrees of success. Most of the people I've met who claim to have achieved this state of mind and being also explain in detail the therapy program they need to maintain it. Jack just chose appreciation as his attitude and from that moment on, he *was* living appreciation.

When I first got to know Jack, I had so many questions for him: "How did you do it? What motivated you? Is it a struggle to find something to appreciate every day?" I interrogated him like a cub reporter, taking notes on how this ordinary mortal had made it across the "appreciation" finish line without sixteen yoga seminars and one spiritual avatar. His answers to me were pure gold, and they have not tarnished in the slightest over a lifetime. Jack explained, "It's been easy for me to find something to appreciate every day. I gave up expectations. Tomorrow doesn't have to be better than today for me in order to have a good day. I don't have to have all my dreams come true in order for me to decide my life is good. I don't care if I don't drive a certain car or have everything I want. I don't want that much. So, it's easy to appreciate life. I took the burden away from God that he had to provide everything for me so I could be happy. Oddly enough, I'm happier now than when I lived possessed by having life turn out my way. People ask me, 'How come you're so happy?' as if I'm on to something. I just decided to choose to see good somehow in people and to appreciate what each day might have in store for me. It makes for a better life."

I have never stopped drawing upon Jack's wisdom as a source of strength. Jack himself made "choice" seem so easy. He didn't anguish, struggle, and sweat over whether his course was the right one or the wrong one. He didn't concern himself with whether, as a result of deciding to appreciate his life, he would lose money or his business edge. He just took a breath, saw the spiritual logic of it all, made his choice, and built a new life. Jack basically is a living Buddha. He has realized at a deep level that "attachment"—to things, people, ideas, expectations—causes suffering and prevents happiness or appreciation. He is living in alignment with Buddha's noble truths: "Life is suffering. Attachment is the source of suffering. The end of attachment will bring the end of suffering." Bless him.

We don't see things as they are, we see them as we are.

— ANAÏS NIN

The maxim "You create your own reality" is the backbone of human consciousness. It's an essential realization to bring into every aspect of your life. Let me make clear, however, that "creating your reality" is not the simplistic desire to make things go your way; it's not a Pollyanna-ish view that sugar-coats events. We each choose to participate in the greater reality that the heavens have created and, like Jack, we each have the power to choose how to respond to every situation in which we find ourselves. How you influence and shape your reality is overseen by your sixth chakra, the center of your mental energy. In this power point, your mind and spirit come together; all of your beliefs, fears, hopes, attitudes, memories, talents, and intellectual skills negotiate multiple planes of reality and perception.

The sixth chakra is located in the center of your forehead, slightly above the midpoint of your brows, where spiritual traditions and art depict the "third eye." Also called the mystical eye of Shiva, the sixth chakra represents intuition or direct cosmic vision and is involved in clairvoyance—second sight. Some animals still have a functional third eye, the pineal gland, which was the first type of eye to develop in vertebrates (so along with a physical spine we developed intuition—the energy that connects us to our spiritual backbone). The pineal gland's cells contain the same kind of light-sensitive cells found in the retina, but its exact function today is unknown, although it still appears to receive signals from regions of the brain involved in sight. This primitive third eye was probably functional before our present two eyes formed and became dominant and it most likely still sends information to our brains and bodies, helping us mediate between different physical and other realities.

The eye with which I see God is the same eye with which God sees me.

—MEISTER ECKEHART

Your beliefs and personal history influence your perception of reality. How do you see your place in the world? Do you see other people as basically good? Are you an optimist or a pessimist? Are miracles real or are you on your own "down here"? How you feel about service is strongly influenced by your answers to these questions and by what you see as your purpose in life. Many people expressed their attitudes about life in general in their letters, such as, "I trust just about everyone," and, "I've never had much luck with people showing up when I've needed them, but I am always there for them," and, "I attract help when I need it because I provide help when needed. Like attracts like is a law I depend on." These comments reflect a personal theology or view of reality that forms much of the hardware of your sixth chakra. This mental energy also helps the universe organize synchronistic events around you.

In a moment of synchronicity, events "just happen" to serve our personal needs. Life is governed by the paradox of the divine, which is that while the universe remains an impersonal, mechanistic, and mathematical operating system, each of us is somehow intimately guided. Our intuition is one way that we in Earth School experience divine intervention. Dramatic stories of rescues are obvious examples of synchronicity, but there are other, more subtle examples. For instance, the imparting of wisdom to someone just at the right moment is every bit as divinely coordinated as is the tow truck that just happened to turn onto the street where you were stuck; it may lack the suspense of a roadside rescue, but it, too, is synchronistic.

But you are in charge of how you see the moments of your life and how you interpret and appreciate them. Writes June X.: "A stranger who was also an astrologer did my chart. After completing my astrological reading, he said, 'June, you really are okay. You really are good enough.' All my life I had felt like I wasn't but as soon as he said that to me, I said, 'I know' and he said, 'Do you?' I left and went out to my car and wept because for the first time I realized that not only was I good enough, I was really, really good, and smart and intuitive. Since that very day, I have been a different person. I believe the acts of service I do are of this same quality. I have the ability to make people feel comfortable and confident, whoever they are. I can and will speak to total strangers, young and old, joke with them and at least for a time, make them feel easy and comfortable with themselves. When you are finally comfortable with yourself, a whole new world opens up. I believe it's an act of service to love yourself and to show love to others."

On the journey to expand our consciousness, sixth-chakra consciousness lifts you past earthly logic and into symbolic perceptions, which gives you access to a completely different set of rules. Your rational mind might not perceive a solution to a crisis, but your inner wisdom and intuition might be enlisted to kick-start a seemingly miraculous synchronistic event.

One woman, for instance, on her way to deliver extra Christmas presents to a charity, lost her way and phoned for directions, dialing what she thought was the number for the charity. But when she followed the directions, she learned that she had actually been led to an impoverished private home filled with needy children. She had "just happened" to dial the wrong number. That type of synchronicity has divine fingerprints all over it.

Spiritual dialogue with the divine begins in your sixth chakra because this power center holds your belief patterns about the universe in general, the goodness of others, and the possibility of divine intervention. The electricity of faith belongs to the domain of your seventh chakra, while the power of the open mind is the sixth.

The Consciousness of Your Sixth Chakra

All Buddhas and all sentient beings are nothing but the One Mind,
beside which nothing else exists.

— HUANG PO

The key word for the sixth chakra is *wisdom,* which we gain through earthly experience. In fact, the motto for this power is "Seek only the truth." The Christian sacrament of ordination is aligned with this chakra, not as a ritual conferring priesthood but as an archetype that represents your ascension to a personal authority. Symbolically, your personal ordination is the recognition of your unique gifts by others and by an even higher authority.

Jean S. did not use the word *ordination* in her letter, which follows, but is describing exactly this quality of individual authority: "I am best known for 'sensing' other people's stress level and creating an opportunity for them to share their thoughts and feelings with me. I help them to reframe the internal messages they are giving to themselves and of course in turn this releases the pressures they put on themselves. I find that I am much appreciated for this act of service."

The recognition Jean receives from others for the healing use of her special gifts represents that which she is ordained to do in this lifetime—her purpose or Sacred Contract.

The sixth chakra is also the contact point between the divine mind and human thought, the portal to enlightenment and transcendent consciousness, which is the goal of all spiritual pursuits. I love the following section drawn from the Zohar, one of the key books of Jewish mysticism, because it shows us that our consciousness mirrors the perfect ordering of the universe:

> King Solomon took up a nutshell and, studying it, saw an analogy in its layers with the spirits that motivate human desires. He saw that our brain is surrounded by numerous membranes and that the whole world, upper and lower, is also organized on this principle, from the mystic center to the very outermost of all the layers. All are coverings, the one to the other, brain within brain, spirit inside spirit, shell within shell. Following this design, we humans combine brain and membrane, spirit and body, all to the more perfect ordering of the world.

Synchronicity: The Quintessential Invisible Act of Power

One thing life has taught me: if you are interested, you never have to look for new interests. They come to you. When you are genuinely interested in one thing, it will always lead to something else.

—ELEANOR ROOSEVELT

The following story is a lovely expression of synchronicity. Many people can relate to the seeming ordinariness of this experience, yet to my mind its commonness makes it all the more extraordinary. Writes Gloria A., "I have a dear friend I don't always have the opportunity to see. However, she always appears at my door or calls just when I seem to need her most, and I do the same for her. Both she and I have done this with many other people as well. I call it my 'gut reaction.' If I cannot get in touch with the person, I usually pray for him or attempt to visualize him in a positive mode. Because I believe thoughts are things, a positive view sent his way could be helpful. I am also someone who believes, when I believe it, I will see it."

Heaven coordinates small and large wonders in our lives— calls from someone we were just thinking about; running into an old friend or colleague unexpectedly. It's one thing to follow a feeling to pick up the phone and call someone, but it's quite another to receive intuitive instructions to channel a message, as happened in the next story.

Barbara M. wrote: "Service has come to mean for me a willingness to follow guidance. On one warm summer day, I was out walking and saw a teenage boy crying with his head down on a table outside a fast-food place. I walked over to him and heard myself say, 'I know your mother is in the hospital and you are afraid that she is going to die, but she isn't going to die for many years yet. She will be better in about three days and ready to come home in two weeks.' The boy was grateful and wanted to hear more. I had to tell him that Spirit had wanted to relieve his mind about his mother but there was no further information. I told him that when information came to me in this way, it was never wrong."

The coordination of a synchronistic event requires an enormous amount of energy. You increase the frequency of synchronistic experiences in your life if you make it a practice to live in present time. As a medical intuitive, I have learned that people who are stuck in the past are hampered in their ability to live and to make decisions. They can't retrieve their energy from their history, and their lack of energy keeps their minds, bodies, and spirits from working together; it also makes them slower to heal. To have your spirit spread out across forty years of history, still "processing" experiences that are decades old, drains your life force. I call this "psychic weight," and the more psychic weight you have in your mind and heart, the longer you have to "wait" for things to happen in your life, including spontaneous forms of assistance coming to you when you need it. When your past is more alive and real to you than the present, synchronistic events are less likely to come together, if for no other reason than you lack the power to recognize them or take advantage of their appearance. A man once told me about a conversation over lunch with a friend during which he said that if the opportunity came to forgive a particular individual in his life, he would jump at it. No sooner had he said that than the person walked into the restaurant where he and his friend were having lunch. The person he was dining with said, "Well, here's your chance. You just got what you prayed for." To his great regret, however, he chose not to accept this divinely coordinated setup, because, as he put it, he was "not prepared to act that fast."

Most people respond immediately and gratefully to such coincidences. You have to be willing to seize the day—to see, accept, and use synchronicities as they present themselves. You would not think twice about accepting a helping hand with a flat tire, for instance, so why turn down a cosmically choreographed opportunity to make amends with someone?

Synchronistic events are not just emergency interventions; they are also a creative force, opening new worlds and opportunities. This letter is another incredible story that reveals the universe's healing nature. Writes Erma B.: "About a year ago, I received a telephone call soliciting donations for a charitable organization. A woman introduced herself, saying, 'This is Jane D. calling on behalf of . . . ' After my initial surprise at hearing her name, I smiled to myself and said, 'Jane, this is Linda.' Then she recognized my voice and we proceeded to catch up. I had become very close to Jane in the aftermath of the Oklahoma City bombing of the federal building. She had lost two young family members in the bombing. It was immediately apparent to me that this reconnection over the phone was not a coincidence. As a result, I now take Jane to a gifted healer on a regular basis who lives an hour and a half away. I feel it is part of my Sacred Contract to be an avenue of healing for her. This is also an opportunity for me to complete some unfinished business around the OKC bombing."

I've actually had people complain that the help they received was "just not enough." Yet since the ancient Greeks, we've quoted the saying, "God helps those who help themselves." The gods will meet us at least halfway, but they will also leave room for us to pull our end of things—to exercise our faith, will, and intention. It is always up to us to choose to recognize a challenge as an opportunity put in our path. Many of the crises in our lives are divinely scheduled to get us to head in another direction. No one gets off a comfortable couch. We need stress, often an enormous amount of it, to muster up the willpower finally to try something new with our lives. As the author and psychiatrist M. Scott Peck writes, "The truth is that our finest moments are most likely to occur when we are feeling deeply uncomfortable, unhappy, or unfulfilled. For it is only in such moments, propelled by our discomfort, that we are likely to step out of our ruts and start searching for different ways or truer answers."

I love the following story from Valerie V. because it illustrates the willingness to take the help offered and believe in it even when it does not seem immediately useful. "Several years ago, I went through a desperate time. I had to move out of the house I had intended to buy. This meant moving my young son into a tiny rental place and giving my beloved dog to my brother hundreds of miles away. I was devastated. In addition, my ex-husband quit his job and stopped paying child support and then my car stopped running for good. After figuring expenses, I still needed three hundred dollars more a month to survive and had no idea where this money was going to come from or even how I was going to get to work.

"I should mention here that I have been very lucky in my life to know the truth and power of prayer. I never doubt that my prayers are heard and answered. I consider this inner knowing a gift from God and have had many instances when my prayers were answered instantly. Unfortunately, during this period of grief I felt like God had let me down and I began to have my doubts. Around this time, I heard Father Malachi Martin interviewed on the radio. I knew instantly he was a man of God. Uncharacteristically I wrote to him and explained that I had been a professional singer for many years and that I wasn't sure if I was in the right place. I don't really remember much more of the letter except to say that I was reaching out for a lifeline of some sort. Father Malachi wrote back and told me he felt certain I was to be his 'special bard' and to 'Get to it!' This was an unexpected response to say the least and I remember thinking that I had no idea how to sing for God or even where to begin. You can imagine my surprise when I received a call from a musician friend who asked if I was interested in being the lead singer in a church gig. I should mention that this possibility had never entered my mind. Anyway, I sang in the church for the next four and a half years. Oh, and like the rest of the band, I was paid three hundred dollars a month. The act of service Father Malachi provided me with was that he prayed for me. He never said so, but I knew to the core of my being that he had. My faith was restored."

When you're stuck, you may need a divine intervention to get your spirit back into the here and now. Whenever something "goes wrong," and something always does, take a deep breath and ask yourself, "Where is my energy? I need to be fully present. I need my energy in the here and now and I need immediate intervention." And then let your prayer go. Allow the laws of attraction and cause-and-effect to pull together a synchronistic response. Let the universe provide you with an invisible act of service.

The Imparting of Wisdom

No one lights a lamp and hides it in a jar or puts it under a bed.
Instead, he puts it on a stand, so that those who come in can see the
light. For there is nothing hidden that will not be disclosed, and
nothing concealed that will not be known or brought out into the open.

—LUKE 8:16–17

Part of the reason we have these experiences in Earth School is to gather wisdom from helping others and from being helped, from both challenging and happy life experiences. Wisdom is the spiritual gold of your sixth chakra. Wisdom transcends the personal, illusion-filled mind and sees the greater truth. I have chosen letters that show that acts of service evolve from visible—physical—help, as in lending a hand, to the invisible—spiritual—help of love and knowledge, the hand of God.

During the course of writing this book, in a conversation with an acquaintance I asked, "What would you prefer to have, a million dollars in cash or a million-dollar piece of wisdom?" With a smirk and a laugh, he responded, "The wise choice would be to take the money." But my question wasn't so much a test as an inquiry into his values. And he gave me a second-chakra valuation of wisdom.

Do you value wisdom? Does wisdom influence your decision making? Have you ever asked yourself, "What is the best, wisest way I can be of service? What can I share with this person that would make a difference beyond this moment?"

Wisdom at the sixth-chakra level can sometimes occur spontaneously, in a sudden awakening or epiphany, when understanding suffuses your being. An epiphany shifts your consciousness from wondering what choice to make to knowing instantly what to do. Another way to think of instant knowing is as an experience of congruence, where all the forces of your consciousness harmoniously come together. The effect is transformational. This happened to the astronaut Edgar Mitchell, who, while viewing the Earth from space, felt a shift in consciousness in which he saw humanity as "one." As if he were a shaman on a journey to inner space rather than a traveler to outer space, his insight moved him from accepting the simple philosophical truth into a full mind-body-spirit knowing and reality. This gnostic or instant knowing changed his life and, back on Earth, he founded the Institute for Noetic Science, to explore and help others explore the parameters of consciousness.

Some letter writers recounted awakenings that were similarly instantaneous and that also became touchstones for their life's path. Writes Jan B.: "When I was nine years old my Camp Fire leader noticed me waiting patiently at the end of line for a chance to build an ice cream sundae. When I got close to the ice cream counter, she thanked me for my patience. Being praised for being patient by my Camp Fire leader surprised and delighted me. I can still recall my feeling of pride. Her compliment fueled my awareness that it is not only good to be patient, it's also good to notice others who are and to verbalize appreciation for their consideration. As a substitute teacher, I find lots of opportunities to praise kids for being patient. I praise them for holding the door open for others and for being good listeners and for contributing harmony to the class. When we boil it all down, I believe our acts of service are about honoring and respecting each other with a deep-seated desire to do unto others as you would have them do unto you. My Camp Fire leader taught me that over thirty years ago."

Jan continues to pass along this simple wisdom to hundreds of children. She is mindful of what she represents as well as what she does in her archetypal role as a teacher. That quality of mindfulness is itself an invisible act of power. We all associate people with their roles. You are you, as you see yourself, but you are also a friend, a coworker, a boss, a mother, or a father; these are archetypes with which people engage whenever they are with you. Being mindful of the power you carry in your many roles will help you become emotionally and spiritually congruent.

The teacher archetype holds incredible power and authority. Parents and teachers are *the* formation team of our youth and without a doubt, part of the tribal carriers of wisdom. Writes Martin T.: "I was a bad kid, no doubt about it. My parents had a lousy marriage and due to their own problems did not have time to look after my younger brother and me. Thinking back, I believe the reason I became a gang member was that I felt a need to be a surrogate role model for my younger brother. I wanted him to feel safe because I knew he was feeling as fragile as I was. Part of the gang 'thing' is to fail in school. I mean, how can you be a respectable gang member and be a good student? These do not go hand in hand. Then one day, my math teacher told me to stay after class. Naturally I thought I was going to get a lecture or a demerit but instead he told me that I had incredible potential to be a mathematician or a scientist. I remember laughing in his face, but at the same time I experienced a feeling of pride that practically exploded in me. No one, and I mean no one, had ever paid that type of attention to me, much less complimented my intelligence. A few days later, I stayed after class because I wanted to talk with him again. How did a person go about becoming a mathematician? He offered to tutor me in math so I could catch up with the advanced classes. He told me that if I did well enough, he would have me transferred to the advanced math classes the following year. Then he added that I would probably do better socially if I dropped out of my gang. That actually ter-rified me because these were tough guys. But that summer, little by little, I removed myself from the gang. Of course they noticed and asked me what was going on with me and I always managed some excuse as to why I wasn't hanging out with them any more. When school began that autumn, obviously they noticed that I was no longer in class with them but had gone into the advanced program. I didn't know if I was going to catch hell or be let alone. Thankfully they just left me alone and I turned all my energy into academics for the first time in my life. This teacher became not only my tutor, but my advisor, my confidant, and now my friend. I am now completing my doctorate in math and I owe it all to this one man who saw a spark of life in a kid from a bad home with a bad attitude. I hope to go on to teach and hope that I can become half the teacher to other kids that he was to me."

Conscious thought truly is power. The wisdom of many spir-itual traditions encourages us to live by that truth, but it always helps to have even more proof, which is why I love the following letter from Sabrina C.: "Three years ago, I was diagnosed with breast cancer and went through breast reconstruction. I also had eight courses of chemotherapy. During that time I received many cards and letters of love, support, and prayers. I also re-ceived a tremendous number of cards and letters from people who I have never met. It touched me so much to know that peo-ple all over were praying for me, including people I didn't know. Prior to that I have to admit regretfully that I would much rather have received a gift or material token of appreciation. It lifts my spirits to realize that I am deeply loved and people prayed for me who didn't even know me. I kept all the cards. They are my trea-sures. And today whenever I am down in the dumps for whatever reason, I remember the power of prayer and all the love and sup-port that came to me during that time. I would much rather have that love and prayers than tokens of appreciations. So in turn, I send cards of love and support to others or offer up a prayer for everyone on the planet many times a day."

Passing the Torch

Reasoning beings were created for one another's sake; and patience is a branch of justice.

—MARCUS AURELIUS

Perhaps the greatest act of service you can perform is the nurturing of your own spiritual path. How we cope with our personal crises can inspire others. Grace is highly attractive. We are drawn to the love, faith, and endurance that others display and we seek out people who have triumphed over a tragedy because the grace in their energy fields lifts us up. This first story has that inspiring quality.

Writes Barb: "My daughter Stephanie drowned in our backyard swimming pool. She was only eight months old. As we were busy preparing for her and her twin's christening day, Stephanie pulled herself past our screen door, managed to get through the pool gate, and into our pool. I had left the gate open for just a few minutes in order to get the wheelbarrow through to the front yard. In those few minutes she did what we thought was impossible for a baby who had not yet learned how to crawl. Our lives were completely shattered. Sammy, her twin sister, got us through. We held onto her and to each other for dear life. And we made it through together, and together we built a new and meaningful life. Service is what helped me survive. Service to others is what kept me going. Service is what helped transform me into the person I believe I was meant to be. Service has been my healing, my direction, and my salvation.

"A few months after Stephanie died, I started doing things I had never thought of before, things that just popped into my head. During our first Christmas without her, I shopped for a family that was in financial difficulty and signed the gift tag, "From your Christmas Angel, Stephanie." I realized doing this made me feel good and I hadn't felt good in a long time. Since then, each day I look for ways of serving others. It has become an unbelievable journey that has taken me to a place I never imagined I would be. I now share my journey with audiences and I love the feeling that comes with sharing. Not long ago, I was standing on a beach looking out to the water and sky. There was such a feeling of awe that came over me. I felt totally connected to God. I said out loud, 'How did I get here?' and instantly the answer came back to me: my daughter Stephanie brought me here.

"Let me add this sweet incident with my son, Scott. I always say a prayer for the person in the ambulance that drives by or if I pass an accident on the street, and I have taught my children to do the same. A couple of weeks ago, we were out for a family bike ride. My ten- and eight-year-old were getting too far ahead and I was starting to panic. I was urging my three-year-old, Scott, to hurry up and as he was not cooperating, I was yelling at my other kids to slow down. I didn't even hear the siren. I looked back and Scotti had hopped off his bike. I was about to scream at him to get back on his bike and join us when I saw him put his hands together. In spite of the moment and my screaming voice, my three-year-old had hopped off his bike and was saying a prayer for the people in trouble."

You can always tell the difference between "wisdom earned" and "wisdom read," so when you have the chance to learn from "wisdom earned," take it. That is the reason why I chose this next letter from Mama Faye: "I'm sixty-six years old. I was dying of a terminal, slow-moving cancer and now, after five years, I'm the picture of health. By choice!!! Knowing that I can create or cocreate what I want in my life, I learned about self-healing and all the energies that help us become whole again. My husband—he's the real healer—encouraged me so much. And now the cancer is gone and I'm not! Then I had a stroke. That was the stick that broke the wagon. I became fighting mad. I just decided to change my mind and here I am today, teaching others to heal themselves. I provide them with Reiki attunements and any other tools I have, including loving my relationship with the creator, loving my work, loving life because I have life and can prove how beautifully energy, light, and love work."

After the double whammy of cancer and stroke, some people might be inclined to think, "Maybe it is my time to go," or, "I must really have stored up some warehouse of negativity." But instead, Mama Faye's response was to become "fighting mad," which helped her heal. Her story reminds me of Yogi Berra's baseball adage, "It ain't over 'til it's over." These women, like magical Jack, decided to change their reality at a soul level. Countless people are now being served by the manner in which these two women chose to cope with their traumas. I can't imagine anyone thinking, "I've got to get through this nightmare so that I can be an inspiration to others." That's ridiculous. Like Job—a biblical Everyman—we will all suffer tragedies that are unfair, that we don't deserve. We'll feel we are looking in vain for God and learn, perhaps much later, that in any difficulty—even the loss of a child—God is also in that place. Trusting in the unseen, ineffable spiritual purpose behind our soul's journey generates a grace that illuminates the world.

Another example of divine synchronicity is told in this letter from Joanie C.: "I got an unexpected phone call regarding my mom one afternoon when I was the only one home. I had to make a two-hour drive to the hospital. When I got there, they told me that my mother had severe pneumonia and all they could do was make her comfortable. I didn't know what to do or how to deal with it. So I called a friend who happened to be home and near the telephone at a time of day when she is never home. I told her what was happening and she told me that when someone is dying, they need three things: they need to know that you love them; they need to know you forgive them; and they need to know that it's okay with you if they leave now. Calmness descended over me and I was able to convey that wisdom to my brother and sister-in-law and it had the same calming effect on them. The next four days with my mother were the most incredibly moving and meaningful of my life. And those few words of wisdom that my friend was able to convey to me made all the difference."

Life sets up situations for all of us that we would prefer not to be in, but cannot avoid. These are "necessary acts of service," leaving us with the only power we have to get through them—the power to choose our attitude. Writes Sam M.: "A few years ago I departed the computer/high tech world of 30 years to volunteer for the Multiple Sclerosis Association. My daughter has MS. She was diagnosed 10 years ago shortly after her graduation from Marquette. After a few years alone, she returned home when she lost the use of her legs. After a year of struggling with the questions why her, why us (wife and me), I decided to volunteer for the MS Association. I have met so many wonderful people and our lives have changed. It has led to a part-time position with the Association. I visit many people with MS and try to give them encouragement. Sometimes the good doctors, as helpful as they might be, don't make a connection. I try to fill the gap with a few smiles, some conversation, or some alternative news on ways to cope, such as meditation and so on. I try the old PMA way—positive mental attitude. Why do I do it? Well, for one thing, it feels good, even though some cases are very sad. I visited a nine-year-old with severe MS recently. I was crushed to see this little one so distorted by the disease. The second reason is a practical one. No one in this situation knows where to find help. I pass on what I know. There have been times in my life when I didn't respond to someone for whatever reason, usually I was lazy or frightened about expressing feelings. The hurt for not doing anything is so much worse then whatever supposed difficulty I had. It is sometimes too late to act and wishing just doesn't cut it."

Another jewel comes from Karen G., who wrote: "There is not one 'job' on this planet that you can hold in which you are not of service to someone somehow. That understanding changed my perspective and how I move through life. I know that whether I am at work offering a candidate a job, or settling an insurance claim, or giving a stranger on the road directions, I am in service. I am helping someone's life. It is a beautiful and often humbling experience. Through that I learned patience and the ability to give more freely rather than being caught up in my own importance."

Knowledge comes, but wisdom lingers.

—ALFRED, LORD TENNYSON

And finally, the following letter offers a perspective on service that is pure inspiration. Writes Pat S.: "I've heard service called the spontaneous outflow of a loving heart and an intelligent mind. Some say to serve is to love. I think about acts of service as I ask myself why does a flower bloom? Is it because it wants to, or because it just does, or because it reaches for the sun? When thinking about the why of service, I wonder if it is because someone or something needs help, or because the server needs to help or because the server is reaching for the sun. No matter what the reason, blooming occurs when service is given and received.

Seeds are sown, lamps are lit, and the continuum of giving and receiving flows."

Examining the Heart of Your Sixth Chakra

Although you do not create your own reality, you do indeed influence it. You improve your health and your life in being of service to others. While I have never told a person during an intuitive reading that his or her stress was due to an inability to help others, I now think such feedback could be useful in some cases. It is far more stressful to your physical and spiritual anatomy to hold back an impulse to reach out to someone than to act on it. If you don't believe me, check out the way you feel next time you hesitate to help.

The truth is, we live in a very public universe—even when we act anonymously. There aren't any secrets, cosmically speaking, and we are observed and used. Next time you find yourself in a giving role, ask yourself, "How did I get here?" and then just assume someone other than you took care of those details.

The following questions are meant for serious self-examination:

<u>As a Giver:</u>
1. Do you follow your own advice and wisdom?
2. When your mind is not occupied with a specific task, do your thoughts tend to wander into the "fear" zone in your mind or do you effortlessly find yourself thinking about your blessings?
3. Are you open to the universe directing you in terms of serving others?

4. List ten things you value about yourself.
5. What do others value most in you?

As a Receiver
1. Do people tend to help you more with thoughts (wisdom) or with things?
2. Have you ever gotten synchronistic help?
3. Does your reality include a belief that you are looked after?
4. How could you change your attitudes to serve your own life and health?

A SIXTH-CHAKRA PRAYER

I release from my mind fears and destructive patterns of thought that do not support my health and well-being. The highest truth that comes through all spiritual masters is that love and service toward humanity serves the highest good of all, including my own life. I will see everything I do today as an act of service on behalf of others and myself.

Oh God of peace, who hast taught us that in returning and
  rest we shall be saved, in quietness and in confidence shall
  be our strength:
By the might of thy Spirit lift us, we pray thee, to thy
  presence, where we may be still and know that thou
  art God. . . .

PRAYER FOR QUIET CONFIDENCE FROM THE
EPISCOPAL BOOK OF COMMON PRAYER

CHAPTER 7

Gifts of the Spirit

Our soul is one to God,
Unchangeable goodness,
And therefore
Between God and our soul
There is neither wrath nor forgiveness
Because there is no between.

— MEDITATIONS WITH JULIAN OF NORWICH

A n old Hindu legend tells of an ancient time when all human beings were gods. But the people so lacked appreciation of their divine nature, however, that the other gods decided to take it away from them. Brahma, the supreme god, wanted to hide human divinity where people would never find it again, and asked his fellow gods to help him find the best place. One god suggested that they bury human divinity deep in the Earth, but Brahma thought they would surely dig deep enough to find it again. Another god wanted to sink it into the depths of the greatest ocean, but Brahma thought that humans would eventually learn to dive deep enough to find it and take it up again. Another god suggested they store it at the top of the highest mountain, but Brahma knew that people would eventually climb high enough to conquer every peak on Earth. Frustrated, the council of gods decided that there wasn't a single place on Earth that humans wouldn't know and conquer, eventually.

So Brahma himself began to think of ways to hide human divinity. He thought for a long time. Finally, he said, "We cannot hide their divinity on Earth for they are determined to own all the planet. But if we hide their divinity within their own being, they will never think to look for it there."

We humans have been looking for our divinity ever since.

Divine Acts of Service

Now there are varieties of gifts, but the same Spirit; and there are varieties of service, but the same Lord; and there are varieties of working, but it is the same God who inspires them all in every one. To each is given the manifestation of the Spirit for the common good.

— 1 COR. 12:4–7

In preparing to write this book, I delved into sacred texts from around the world, looking for wisdom stories that reflected the timeless values of humanity that are mirrored in the letters people sent me. Immersed in them, I discovered once again, as I had in graduate school when studying for a master's in theology, that you cannot just read inspirational material as if it were history. Sacred scriptures are meant to disrupt their readers' lives and souls in the same way that their writing turned upside down their authors' lives and souls. They draw you deep inside yourself, where you learn about your own vulnerabilities and fears, your capacity for goodness and giving, and then they throw you out again into the world to act in accordance with what you've learned. Again and again, they advise us that we act divinely when we act in service to others.

Over time, the grace we acquire from acts of service and self-understanding becomes part of our nature. Writes Patty L.: "During the 1980s, I was a single mother of two going to school and working as a waitress. There was a family who I'll call the Browns who frequented the restaurant—an older couple along with their son and daughter-in-law. They were kind and decent people, but I never had an extraordinary relationship with them. When I had lulls during my shift, I'd go into the women's room and smoke a cigarette. One time as I was pulling a cigarette out of my pocket, Mrs. Brown walked in. Something struck me profoundly and unexpectedly when I saw her and I slipped my cigarettes back into my pocket. I didn't want her to see that I smoked. It didn't come from some expectation that she would judge me. In fact, quite the contrary, since I felt completely accepted by her. I had the sense that she accepted all people as they were. I recognized that it was who she was, her 'being' that made me want to better myself. She touched something higher in me. I never told her about that experience and the point is that she didn't 'do' anything. It came from who she was—a kind, loving, and genuine person who inspired something higher in me. She put me in touch with my conscience."

Another story of a human angel whose very being had a grace that inspired others is from Kathy M., who wrote, "Once, when I was a security officer at a major hospital, I was walking down a long corridor thinking about what a bad day in Earth School I was having. I looked up and noticed that the only person coming toward me was a mental-health patient. I really was feeling down and wanted to keep my eyes to the floor, but I could feel his energy and noticed that he was staring at me. I could feel more energy going through me as we walked closer to each other. I then noticed the incredible smile on his face as he raised his hand in a 'high-five' position. Not wanting to appear rude, I, too, raised my hand to meet his. As we touched and made eye contact, something very profound happened. I experienced so many 'shifts' take place inside of me. I felt joy rush through my body. This man simply reached out with love, something I could not do that day. He taught me that one human being can deeply affect another by the simplest means. He not only changed my day, he changed my life. Here I am, the 'security officer,' and here was this man, the 'mental health patient,' and he touched my heart when no one else could. I felt so humbled."

This story reminds me of the ancient tradition of "shakti-pat," which literally means "the descent of grace." A guru will transmit spiritual energy to a student or seeker in a physical blessing, usually with a touch on the forehead at the third eye or on the crown of the head. The effect is an instantaneous down-loading of divine energy and an awakening of the spirit within. Biblical Scriptures recount a similar transfer of energy through healing touch, especially in the miracle stories of Jesus. These healings are not "just" physical healing but also spiritual; they are meant to demonstrate the power of the divine at work in our lives, reclaiming us, reawakening our own highest nature. As a result of Jesus' gift of healing touch, people's bodies and souls were made whole *and* holy. We see this same effect in gifts of service.

Jesus healed the blind, sick, lame, and those possessed with demons, and brought back Lazarus from the dead in a kind of re-verse of the sacrament of extreme unction or last rites. This Christian ritual is commonly associated with the anointing of a dying person in preparation for the soul's meeting with God, yet we can see it as having another, symbolic meaning: the re-claiming of your spirit from the past, from that which has already died in your life, in preparation for a new beginning in life, a resurrection of your spirit. In the realm of the seventh chakra, spiritual awakenings are common. Many people who wrote me letters described the gifts of service they received as life changing and as awakening them to greater meaning and purpose in their lives.

In a sense, we ourselves become embodiments of invisible acts of power when we respond naturally and automatically with love, compassion, and kindness to people around us. Then we are acting from the power of the seventh chakra, the divine impulse, with which we are likely to create miracles every day.

The Consciousness of Your Seventh Chakra

God is love, and he who is in love is in God and God in him.

—MEISTER ECKEHART

The seventh chakra is in fact the house of miracles—manifestations of the purest form of the energy of grace. This center also contains unbridled mystical power. Observers traditionally kept their distance from those medieval mystics who were known to have made direct contact with Heaven—even if they lived together in a monastery—lest the "eye of the divine" blink in their direction; few are strong enough to endure that daily, direct, electric current. In the Scriptures, however, miracles were often referred to as wonders or signs that point to the divine at work "on Earth as it is in heaven."

In the dimension of the seventh chakra, our consciousness and spirit can have a conscious rapport and personal spiritual connection with the divine. Here, we "live in the present moment," which is the motto of this chakra, and which makes all our energy available for high-voltage, miraculous connections. All the wonderful acts of service that people have shared in this book contain a quality of spiritual grace, but some point directly at divine influence. In the following story, for example, Christopher tells of an angelic intervention in a serious accident.

He writes: "By my mid-forties I was drifting more and more into a numbness of mind and spirit. The only way I could connect with life was through that adrenaline rush racing motorcycles and balancing on that fine line between life and death. Now this is a very seductive high—a mistress one pays dearly for. I lived from high to high not seeing the beauty in the ordinary or feeling a sense of gratitude for just being alive. All this changed one beautiful moonlit night on a lonely country road. The moon was so bright that I was awestruck. I was traveling at double the posted speed limit on a motorcycle that felt as if it were a mere extension of my thoughts. Man and machine were one and adrenaline flooded my senses. Through this trance I caught the reflection of two eyes—a deer's—glowing in the bushes. Time started to slow down; it was as if some power were taking over. I knew this was my destiny on that beautiful night. The deer responded as if on cue and started charging across the road. I slammed on the brakes and we collided at eighty miles per hour.

"The sound was horrific. The flight into midair was wrenching and the motorcycle cartwheeled. Then we all lay silent. The deer was dead, the motorcycle was a wreck, but I was still alive. I couldn't breathe let alone move and I was in the middle of the road. As I lay there a voice—that inner guiding voice—kept affirming, 'You will be fine.' It was dark, and I was dressed in black leather, impossible for an oncoming car to see. I thought, 'Did I survive the crash only to be hit by a car?' I heard a car approaching. Then I heard the door slam and the sound of purposeful footsteps coming toward me. It felt like grace descending as she spoke, her voice calm but authoritative. Her presence was so reassuring. I will never forget the feeling of her compassion. This beautiful spirit from out of the night orchestrated my rescue and subsequent transportation by helicopter to a local trauma unit.

While in her presence, I felt the outpouring of love and security, and as I was taken from her side, the night became truly cold and painful. I have never really believed in angels, but I met one that night. Though I never saw her face, I know her love. Months later I tried to find her. I searched the police reports and I found no mention of her. It's as if I was the only one who knew that she had been there at the scene. This was an angel who came to comfort me in my time of need, who taught me to trust in another, and who demonstrated the marvelous ways Spirit works.

"My life took on a new meaning and purpose. I sold the motorcycle and I am grateful to the deer and the part she played in my awakening. My perspective toward life truly shifted. Spirit works to awaken us and it seems that if we don't attention to the subtle messages, the messages increase in volume and severity. On the very day of the crash, I had been warned to slow down by a rabbit crossing my path. I remember how close I was to crashing then and how strange it was to see an animal act in this fashion. Now I know that this was a sign to slow down and pay more attention. I am grateful for the crash and I will never call it an accident because of the profound gift it provided. Years have passed and I remain grateful to be able to breathe and walk and to share my love with others."

The seventh chakra's energy is transpersonal, aligned to spiritual transformation. Christopher's life was not just saved by his angel; she—and his accident—led to his profound spiritual awakening.

After I shared Christopher's story in a workshop, a student asked, "How come he got an angel and I just got a neighbor helping me?" Between the lines of that question also lurk the questions "How come help didn't come to me when I needed it?" and "Where is God when *I* need him or her?" I have also been asked if there is some sort of "special prayer" that goes to the head of the line in heaven, a type of prayer that would put things right in our lives just when we need it most. I can only say what I believe—no prayer goes unanswered. Some prayers take a bit more time to manifest; and some answers just take more effort for *you* to detect. Even when our prayers *appear* not to have been answered, we can be sure that they *have* been received and that an answer is already here or on the way. Perhaps that answer does not come at the moment of the prayer or in a personal form that we recognize or an angelic presence that we would like to see. But answers to our prayers filter into physical manifestation when the time is right. It is up to us to notice them. Two people can have a stranger help them pay for their groceries, but each will interpret the gesture differently. One person may see it as simple kindness and the other may see the hand of the divine at work. How we choose to interpret our experiences is up to us, but those choices very much influence our vision of God. Some people view their intuition as a sixth sense; others as divine guidance. Heaven appears to us in ways that we can recognize and understand.

Sai Baba, the great contemporary Hindu mystic who manifests holy ash out of thin air and spontaneously heals people, teaches that we cannot see why help and healing seem to come to some people and not others. Only the most highly evolved spiritual master can see deep enough into karma to perceive the divine reasoning behind the heavens' acts. And what he or she sees cannot be explained in terms of human logic, so we cannot look for explanations. Even the seventh chakra's Sanskrit name, which means the "unqualified absolute," indicates the impossibility of defining the nature of God.

Yet every human being longs for life to be a "controlled substance," a logical, organized, rational experience in which our prayers are answered as we would like them to be answered. But heaven has never wrapped itself around our needs; rather, our needs lead us to trust in heaven, to build our faith.

Invoking the Divine

All things are possible to him who believes.

—MARK 9:17–24

The key word to the seventh chakra is *faith* and its greatest power is prayer, which is for me the purest invisible act of power. With prayer, we invoke the divine. The seventh chakra is the portal through which divine energy enters into our individual consciousness. I often refer to the seventh chakra as our "grace bank account" because I believe we do accumulate or warehouse grace as a result of our actions and thoughts.

Stories about prayer and divine intervention reminded me of a visit to a Carmelite convent when I was eleven years old. We were only allowed to view the kitchen, a nun's cell, and the general meeting room, but I was greatly impressed with the stark white walls of the corridor and the pristine, clean floors. But what I remember best was the answer the reverend mother gave me when I asked, "But what do you *do* here all day? I mean, you can't leave or talk to anyone. So, what do you *do?*" She said, "We pray for those who cannot or do not pray for themselves. We pray for the world." Her words had an electrifying, physical effect on me and they seared themselves into my memory. Now, many years since that formative exchange with the reverend mother, I can see that the power of prayer and intention—theirs, yours, mine—forges the grace that holds our world together.

Many people set aside a part of their daily schedule to pray for others. Some wrote me that they say a prayer for everyone they work with, whether that work is one-on-one therapy sessions or in an office building. The following letter affirms the power of conscious prayer. Writes Rich L.: "I am an awesome massage therapist. At the end of a massage treatment, I generally wind up with the person lying in a supine position and I finish with the head of the person cradled in my hands and forearms. At that time, I say a silent prayer of thanks for the ability to work with that person and ask that they be watched over and protected. This one time, as I got up to leave the session, the client said, 'Thank you for the prayers.' I was completely taken by surprise because I had not uttered a word. I had prayed in silence, yet she knew I had prayed for her. That made the hair on the back of my neck stand straight up. We do and can make a difference."

And in a very sweet and simple letter, Tom D. writes, "When I see people who are suffering emotional pain, trapped by a world filled with external distractions or just completely devoid of spirit, I send them love and light and a prayer of comfort. Sending love and healing energy to others is wonderfully effective."

The next stories demonstrate that at our lowest point of desperation, loneliness, or panic, a divine energy can manifest in response to our plea. Writes Pat A.: "A few years ago I was going through a very painful divorce. My soon to be ex-husband was doing his best to destroy my reputation since I was the one who filed. Worse than that was how all of this was affecting my children. Many nights I went to our church chapel and I would sit there until the middle of the night. I started bringing a small pillow with me because sometimes I would get so tired from crying that I would have to close my eyes for a bit. One night I was in the chapel crying as I had done many times before, but I was at my breaking point. I was angry because I could not stand to see my children hurt and I could do nothing to protect them. I had been praying and then I started to weep. I told God, 'I need help and I need it *right here and right now, right this minute because I can't handle one more minute of this alone.'*

"With that, I took the pillow and threw it against the wall of the chapel. I sat in the front pew crying. I didn't have the strength to get up and retrieve my pillow. Immediately the door at the back of the chapel opened and a woman walked in. Usually when someone goes into church and sees anyone praying, they stay back and given them space. Not this woman. She marched right up to the front pew, sat down, and put her arm around my shoulder. She started talking to me and everything she said made so much sense. I felt the presence of peace sweep over me. How could she have known what was going on in my life? I had never seen this woman, yet she spoke to me as if she had been walking with me the entire last year through this divorce. As I calmed down, I looked at her and said, 'I don't even know you, but I feel like I do. I have never seen you before. I don't even know your name.' She hugged me and replied, 'My name is Grace.' I remember thinking, 'Well, doesn't that just about figure?' With that she got up and left after she told me that I would be fine. I have never seen her since and I will never forget that evening. I know if you ask for help you get it, but that was really quick. I didn't even say please, but I have definitely said thank you. I came away from that night with new strength and renewed faith. I have never again been as hopeless as I was before Grace came into my life."

Denise G. also shared a version of a "grace" story: "When my children were babies, I was stranded in the suburbs without a car and not within walking distance of anyplace. A neighbor called frantically asking if I would lend her a particular brand of baby food for her highly allergic, sick child. I did not have what she needed and she could not use what I had. My friend became hysterical, explaining that she had given the last of her money to a child to go to the store on her bike and pick up the food. The child returned with two broken jars, explaining that she had dropped the food on the way back. I told my friend that I would have the food for her in thirty minutes. Then I hung up the phone wondering how I would make that happen. No adults were home in the neighborhood. I stood looking out the front door and prayed, 'Lord, I need inspiration, now!' Just then I saw two grade-school-age kids walking down the street toward my house. They asked me if I had any chores they could do to earn a little money! I asked if their parents would allow them to ride to the grocery store on their bikes. They could and they did. They delivered the baby food to our neighbor just as the baby was awaking from her nap. Now at no time before or ever again did kids ring my bell asking to do a chore for a dollar, but they did at the very moment I had committed to doing something I had no way accomplishing without this miracle. I believe it took my unqualified promise to deliver a specific result and asking for divine intervention that made the miracle happen."

Writes Amy B.: "After my boyfriend broke up with me, I was devastated. I walked away crying and sat down on a bench. A woman came up to me and said, 'It's important to have a shoulder to cry on. You don't need to tell me your problems, but after you're done, you'll be fine. I see you're sad, but remember, God is with you no matter what you do.' This was a total surprise and when I got up after saying thank you, she was nowhere in sight. Yet I felt assured by her that I would be okay and that breaking up was the right decision."

The Power of Smile Yoga

Remember that you have only one soul; that you have only one death to die; that you have only one life, which is short and has

to be lived by you alone; and there is only one glory which is eternal. If
you do this, there will be many things about which you care nothing.
— ST. TERESA OF ÁVILA, *MAXIMS FOR HER NUNS*

You have probably served a role in a miracle or two and you
don't even know it. We tend to think of miracles as theatrical,
cosmic interventions in the midst of terminal illnesses or other
dramas, but millions of miracles occur each day and, in keeping
with the nature of invisible acts of power, go unnoticed. But as
the Zen master Thich Nhat Hanh has written, "Every day we are
engaged in a miracle which we don't even recognize: a blue sky,
white clouds, green leaves, the black, curious eyes of a child—our
own two eyes. All is a miracle." Thich Nhat Hanh also teaches us
to practice "mouth yoga"—the power of a smile.

Jane L. shared a very simple experience, but not an ordinary
one. She writes: "One day in early 1973, after I had left high
school early and begun working full time before entering college, I was driving along when I suddenly felt completely disconnected from the world. My friends were all still in school but I
didn't feel any connection to them. I had a profound feeling of
being completely alone. As I continued to drive, another car with
a stranger passed by and our eyes met. He smiled and waved a
slight wave of warmth, and that was that. But as a result, I knew I
was not alone in this world and I regained my perspective." This
sweet little miracle reconnected a young girl's spirit to the goodness of life.

Smile story number two is equally tender and suggests,
again, that angels like automobiles. Writes Russell D.: "A number of years ago I was in a state of depression serious enough to
contemplate suicide. I elected to not take any ameliorating drugs
and instead allowed myself to fall into the depths of my own soul.
On one particularly dismal morning, I was about to make my way
across the street when a car approached. Pausing to let the car

pass, the driver instead offered the courtesy of waving me across first. I looked at the stranger behind the steering wheel and saw her smiling at me so warmly. And this was certainly not in return for my smile, because I had none. But I saw her smile and felt it; it lifted me beyond what I ever would have imagined. She seemed like an angel and I doubt that I will ever forget her warmth and the power of a sincere smile for someone in need."

Smile story number three is one more proof that invisible acts of power run through everyone's being, whether or not we are conscious of them. Writes Andrea W.: "I was walking to my car on a day that I was feeling particularly low when a street vendor came up to me. Here in South Africa, we are plagued by street vendors bothering you at every turn by their wares. But that day as I turned to this woman politely refusing her advances, she suddenly beamed the most sweeping, beautiful, and heart-warming smile I have ever seen. Her smile was so genuine and so sincere that her whole face lit up and I knew it came from her very soul. Looking at how shabbily dressed she was I realized she didn't have much in life, but what she lacked in material wealth she certainly made up for in spiritual riches. That spontaneous and simple act lifted my heart and touched my very being and I still feel the effects today when I think about it. I feel truly blessed as I believe the divine reached out to me that day through this wonderful woman when I needed it the most. I can't explain the impression it had on me because how do you put into words the feelings of one's soul reaching out to another spontaneously? I have never seen this woman again. I believe acts of service come in the physically unobtrusive form of prayer. I have proved to myself over and over again how scenes of verbal and physical violations, for example, have been diffused within minutes of a prayer. I have never doubted the power of prayer, but sometimes seeing immediate and tangible proof enhances what we already know to be true deep down."

These visible smiles conveyed invisible power. They were small spiritual and physical miracles. Miracles are in the eyes of the beholder; that is, we define a miracle by its effect on us, but I now consider all goodness to be the stuff of miracles. In my life, I've had a fair number of occurrences that qualify as miracles, too. One time, for instance, I had a horrendous flu and could not make it to a workshop I was scheduled to teach. The group sponsoring the workshop was very sympathetic but they were expecting hundreds of people and were now without a presenter. They asked if I could think of someone—anyone—who could stand in. For some unknown reason, the only person who crossed my mind was a marvelous physician, Dr. Gladys McGarey, who lives in Arizona. Gladys is very dear to me, but we had never taught together and her expertise is pregnancy and childbirth—not exactly my specialty. I gave them her phone number and upon calling her office, they learned she was out of town doing a workshop of her own. When they inquired as to where she was, it turned out she was teaching in the same hotel my seminar was in, and not only that, she was in the room directly across the hall from the one scheduled for my presentation. And further, her workshop was ending just as mine was scheduled to begin, so darling Gladys just walked across the hall and took over. Now that was a miracle and a mega act of service, but so are the wave of a hand and smile from a stranger that reconnect us to the goodness of life. And so is the story told in the following letter.

Jim M. shares: "On July 19, 2003, I wrecked a motorcycle I was riding, or so I'm told. I have no memory of the night or the next five weeks. I had brain surgery to remove blood clots. I had damaged the right side of my head pretty badly. I spent eleven days in a coma and twenty-five more in rehab, of which I also have no memory. My folks and one sister were with me almost every day. Around twenty friends stopped by on my forty-third birthday while I was still in a coma. Three days before my other sister and her husband came to visit, I started a remarkable recovery. We, I should say I, had a great weekend together. I was released ten days later into the care of two friends. Three weeks later, they had a benefit for me and this is what amazed me the most. There were around 180 friends there and I remembered all of them. I hadn't been in touch with some of them for fifteen years. And they all had one thing in common—they were all praying for me. Now do you believe in miracles? I do."

The following two stories illustrate beautifully how the universe drafts us into service to help perform miracles. Writes Michael M.: "On February 17, 1994, I was one of a group of people who were setting out to deliver invitations to a parish renewal mission in Northern Ireland. We were standing outside the church chatting before we went our separate ways. During the conversation, I felt a desire to go inside the church and pray. My prayer was one of thanks for my faith and for my late parents and grandparents who had passed that faith on to me. I then asked God's blessing on me and my undertaking and to make it successful. Sometime later as I delivered the last invitation, a massive explosion went off very close to me. I ran toward the scene and discovered that a police-armed Land Rover had been hit with a propelled rocket. The device had hit the driver's doors so I went to the other side of the vehicle only to discover the passenger was out of the car and pointing his gun straight at me, shouting that he was going to shoot me. The policeman was in a state of shock. He was covered in blood and his hand was trembling. I will always remember the fear in his eyes and looking into the barrel of his gun. I raised my hands in the air and approached him. He calmed down when he realized I was not part of the ambush that had just taken place. I told him to radio for help while I went over to his friend who had been hit. I could only enter the car from the back as the entire inside front was covered with blood and pieces of flesh. The driver was lying across the steering wheel. I lifted him back and held him in my arms. I immediately realized he would never again see his family. As I cradled him in my arms, I told him that Jesus loved him. Suddenly I felt the presence of God within me and at that moment, I felt that God was using my body to hold and comfort this dying man. His friend had told me his name and I kept reassuring him that Jesus loved him. My belief is that those were the last words he would hear in this lifetime and the first he would hear in the next. He was a young Christian man with a young wife and family. His mother told me later of what a consolation it was for them that he did not die alone and that he heard the name of God whispered in his ear. We both came from different sides of the divide and as a result of that day, a group of us—Catholics and Protestants— now meet every month in prayer."

The second miracle story reveals the extraordinary way that the universe weaves us in and out of each other's lives. Writes Paul J.: "In 1982, I was part of a men's group. I was twenty-three years old and looking for direction. There was an older man with a southern accent who seemed to be everywhere I turned. I had shared with him my ideas of God and how I was unimpressed with the Episcopal tradition I grew up in. One evening, he presented me with a bookmark. It had my name on [it] in woven letters along with a Bible quote. I thanked him and when I got home, I put it in a book, and promptly forgot about it. Years later in 1993, my world as I knew it was coming to an end. Everyone, except for my parents, was dying of AIDS. Not a day went by that I wasn't at a hospital for a friend or attending to my own partner. The grief and sadness were overwhelming. I went out for a walk and ended up at the Episcopal Church. The doors were open and I remembered my grandmother's words of comfort, 'If you need anything, God will hear you.'

"I went in. A Tuesday evening service was being held. A

warm feeling flowed over me. As the Communion was being prepared, I realized I had not had Communion in years. I found myself at the Communion rail and as the priest passed in front of me, I burst into tears. I sobbed as the pent-up emotions of so many deaths and so much loss swelled inside of me. This sweet priest lifted my chin and looked into my eyes and said that the Lord knew what I needed and that I was loved deeply. He pressed my wet face against his chest as I continued to cry the cry of the heartbroken. On the walk home, I felt relieved, as if an emotional blister had broken. Upon returning home, the nurse who was attending my partner told me he was sleeping peacefully. I picked out a book from the bookcase and out fluttered the old bookmark. 'Funny,' I thought. 'I wonder what happened to that sweet man who gave this to me.' I was sure he died with all the rest. Later I was telling the story to a friend, who told me, 'Don't you know about the priest? He is the man who gave you the bookmark. He is the priest at St. Thomas Church.'

"I couldn't believe it. I returned to the church and he was indeed the man who had gifted me with that bookmark years earlier. He didn't realize it was me at the Mass and I certainly didn't recognize him. And to find the bookmark that same evening? God does work in paradox. I was reassured and humbled by this experience."

With men it is impossible, but not with God; for all things are possible with God.

— MARK 10:27

As I wrote in the introduction to this book, faith is not passive; it is an active force. And with it we can move mountains. The heavens send us our difficulties and our joys because we need to develop faith: faith that our needs will be met; faith that we are not alone; faith that there is a greater purpose at work behind the scenes that will become known to us when the time is right.

Some people wrote me that they had never received an invisible act of power or even a visible act of service. One said that she has spent the greater part of her life giving to others while rarely if ever experiencing that type of support in return. Why is it, three different people asked, that miracles seem to occur in others' lives and not in their own? Who knows what fields of grace surround us? That our troubles and pain are not immediately resolved to our satisfaction does not mean that we have not received grace and guidance. If we can't yet see into the reasons for why our life has unfolded as it has, perhaps we have not yet been graduated from our mandatory course in developing faith on Earth School.

I love the following story, which I would classify as a miracle, but others might dismiss. Writes Richard H.: "I was at a conference at Stanford University at a particularly bad time in my life. I had many personal problems; divorce, taking my Ph.D. orals— I was a complete emotional basket case. On my way to the men's room at a restaurant, I passed a public telephone where the phone book was lying open to a random page. For some reason I looked at the phone book and was ready to put it back when I noticed a name and a phone number. There was absolutely nothing different about the name and the number that would differentiate it from the others on the page. In fact, it was just two initials and a last name. I linked that to the name of a woman who I had known several years before. I can't even say why I connected it because it wasn't even the same last name that I knew her by. It was her maiden name and I knew her by her married name. I can't even remember how or why I linked the two names together. I dropped a coin in the phone and dialed. She picked up the phone on the second ring and then started laughing, saying that she was just thinking about me. We didn't even know each other that well. We met for lunch. We spent several days together and she taught me so many things that helped me to regain my confidence and feel better. We stayed in touch for a couple of years but I don't know where she is today. I do believe, however, that if I ever need her again, she'll be back."

Angels and Automobiles

You must not lose faith in humanity. Humanity is an ocean; if a few drops of the ocean are dirty, the ocean does not become dirty.

— MAHATMA GANDHI

Automobiles seem to be the vehicle of choice for the universe to place a person in a vulnerable situation and a rescue that turns into a spiritual experience. A car breakdown is not a "seventh-chakra" crisis unless the individuals perceive it as profoundly spiritual. My father, a veteran of World War II and a U.S. Marine, passed on to my brothers and me the old adage "There are no atheists in foxholes." My translation—if heaven can scare you enough, you'll start praying. Car breakdowns also seem to be an ideal setting for the universe to introduce people that need to meet, if only for a few minutes. But in those few minutes, their lives are changed forever.

Carrie's story was one of several about accidents that I received in which invisible helpers showed up and then disappeared after their work was done. Perhaps only an angel could have gotten there on time.

Writes Carrie M.: "I was in a serious auto accident in which I was left injured and trapped in my car. A woman stopped and came to my car, which was a ways off the road at that point. She reached through the broken window to cover me with a blanket and then stood next to me, reassuring me, until the rescue squad came. When they arrived, she disappeared, leaving behind her blanket. I never found out who she was but I think of her often and have always wanted to tell her how significant that act of service was for me and continues to be till this day."

Writes Nicole R.: "One day I ran out of gas on the freeway. I had my two boys in the car and I had managed to roll the car into the stopping lane. I was within a slightly long walking distance to an off-ramp that I knew led to a gas station. I was standing outside the car wondering what to do when a car pulled over and a lady in her late fifties got out. I noticed she had a little boy about twelve months old in the car. She asked if she could be of help and I explained the situation to her. Somehow we got to chatting and she told me she was looking after her grandson and enjoyed teaching him about God. I am spiritual but not religious, however, I could feel this woman's loving energy. She gave me five dollars and when I asked for her address so I could repay her, she said, 'Don't worry about it. I've been there,' and then she got in her car and drove away. It was only five dollars, but to me it was a huge amount as I was able to get fuel and drive home. I hadn't told her that I was broke, but she knew it. I have never forgotten that and always look out for similar situations so I can do the same for them."

Writes Noelle S.: "The car my husband and I were driving broke down outside a little town in South Carolina. Five minutes later a motorist stopped by to help and then the highway safety patrol stopped and towed us to a local mechanic in this little town where the mechanic proceeded to spend all day working on our car. He enlisted the help of another mechanic across town who had to visit two junkyards to find the parts we needed. They worked on our car for five hours so that we could be on our way to our destination, which was about three hours away. The mechanics and junkyard people only charged us for one of two parts from the junkyard and the labor to install only the one part needed. The other part, and the hours of labor by everyone, was free. My husband and I, who were both desperately in need of this minivacation, found we were of one mind after that incident. We didn't care that the breakdown took one whole day out of our short vacation because we felt that we had had a vacation among real humanity that day."

I have another twenty-four examples of "angels and automobiles." The heavens employ all sorts of difficulties—accidents, arguments, car troubles—to get our attention and show us the potential for grace to manifest in our lives. You just never know why things happen as they do or why you end up in the midst of a disaster, but there is something enormously comforting and spiritually compelling in the thought that wherever you are could be a setup for something profoundly mystical to come into your life.

A Walking Miracle:

THE HEALING POWER OF FAITH AND DEVOTION

The seventh chakra represents a level of consciousness in which you can do what has not been done before. And the will to accomplish that draws into your life the help that you need. I have met many, many people in my work who have serious, potentially chronic and terminal illnesses. The woman who is the subject of this letter, Anne B., has multiple sclerosis, yet she has beat the odds. Stories about people who succeed in putting into remission degenerative illnesses need to be shared just because they inspire hope. Anne's story is pure seventh-chakra material because she drew upon a power much greater than herself and in the process, saw her illness as a way to be of service to others. I am very grateful that her massage therapist, Robert C., took the time to write this story because I have no doubt that Anne's spirit will continue to inspire others confronting serious illnesses.

Writes Robert C.: "When I first met Anne, she was strapped into an electric wheelchair with two wide belts cinched tightly around her torso to hold her upright. She wore a neck brace to support her head, which she could barely rotate right or left without pain and muscle spasm. Anne wore splints on both wrists. Her legs lay inert. Her mind was imprisoned in an unheeding body. I had no way of knowing upon meeting Anne that working with her would change our lives and the way I work forever.

"I had just given a talk at a chapter of the Multiple Sclerosis Society. In sharp juxtaposition to her physical appearance, Anne's blue eyes were excited and inquisitive. She asked if I could help her. I had only been out of training for a year, so I was too young and full of missionary zeal to say no. Thursday afternoons were dedicated to Anne. I hauled my massage table out to the car and drove to her home just outside town. I had great compassion for Anne. Morbid MS had taken so much from her. She had faced death and terrible medical trials several times. I had been blessed in life and it appeared Anne had been, by most standards, cursed. Pain was constant. She had been struck with immobility quickly and had three preschoolers at home. She lived with a daily test I knew in my heart I could not have faced, and this was the root of my compassion.

"The first treatment was simple relaxation massage. After the session, I asked about her pain level and she said, 'It's different.' By different, Anne meant that there was no pain. She was astonished and I pretended not to be. Our journey had begun.

Three weeks of every month I worked with Anne. Swedish massages melded into visualization and Reiki. Exercise helped to bring old patterns back or to create new movement patterns where nerves no longer worked. Craniosacral work was key and somatoemotional releases occurred several times per session. There was so much emotional and spiritual conflict to clear away. Anne was determined to heal for her own health and for the good of her family. Even before her healing began she ran her household, raised her children, and was as active as anyone could be working with a body that would not obey her brain's commands. Throughout her long, painful recovery, she continued to act as a person who was not ill. MS ruled her body but not her life. She gained local celebrity as a spokesperson for the MS Society, used the phone to reach out to fellow sufferers, served on numerous committees, and babysat a neighbor's child after school each day. She paid me with the babysitting money she earned.

"Her first sideways step took all of one winter. Through Voice Dialogue techniques, I connected to Anne's inner physician, a plain-speaking entity named Dr. Anne. Anne had been a cancer nurse specialist and Dr. Anne, her inner physician who knew all, often led me through treatments. Together they taught me what I needed to know to clear energetic cysts and facilitate harmonious movement patterns. In the middle of somatoemotional releases revisiting near-drowning memories, birth trauma, and chemotherapy, Anne often looked like she would choke to death. We knew to wait and it would pass. As Anne began to visibly recover, other MS patients began to see that the world was yet full of possibility where the cynicism of others had once stolen hope.

"Thirteen years after she had been paralyzed by MS, nearly a quadriplegic, Anne began to walk again. Then she started getting stronger and stronger. The milestones kept coming. One spring day she was standing by her house and a neighbor pulling into his driveway who had never seen Anne out of her wheelchair, caught sight of her in his rearview mirror and slammed his car right into his garage door. Anne traveled all the way to Israel to receive a humanitarian award for her work with the MS Society. Later that year she decided she wanted to drive again. I tried to dissuade her because of my concern about her reaction time. She earned her driver's license without any problems and I decided not to worry about her driving. Then she sold her wheelchair. There was no going back.

"Eventually Anne could drive to my office, but she had to pull herself up the steep flight of stairs. She had to do this sitting down. I can think of so many other clients who would not have risen to that challenge and thought it undignified. Anne had lots of problems, but she was never burdened with a misplaced sense of entitlement. I couldn't go to her, so she came to me, no matter what it took. The trips up and down the stairs became part of her rehabilitation program. The following spring, Anne walked three kilometers in a fund-raiser for the MS Society.

"Today Anne is a healer of meteoric insight and skill. Anne is a walking miracle. She is now a colleague and thanks to her I have a new definition of 'friend.' A friend is someone whose presence inspires and elevates you to be the best you can be."

Examining the Heart of Your Seventh Chakra

Your seventh chakra represents that place in your life where you and the divine meet. This is your point of light, your grace reservoir, your spiritual life. Rather than closing this chapter with questions as I have in the previous ones, I want to leave you with two prayers that beautifully embody the essence of spiritual union with the divine.

A SEVENTH-CHAKRA PRAYER

"May I be open and present to all guidance that directs me to be of spiritual support to others. And when I am in need of support, please direct me to those who You would select on my behalf. I remain forever grateful that You so closely and lovingly keep a mindful eye on all of us who share life on this earth. So often we do not understand why we must endure what is asked of us; in those times, grant me the grace of faith. May I always be guided to live a life of service that benefits humanity and the quality of my own spiritual journey."

The Light of God before me.
The Light of God behind me.
The Light of God above me.
The Light of God beside me.
The Light of God within me.

— FROM THE PRAYER OF ST. PATRICK

CHAPTER 8

Invisible Facts
of Power

Have benevolence toward all living beings, joy at the sight of the virtuous, compassion and sympathy for the afflicted, and tolerance towards the indolent and ill-behaved.

— TATTVARTHASUTRA 7:11 (JAINISM)

Years ago I had a conversation with a man who told me that the most important truth he had learned was to be kind. He learned this, he recounted, during a cab ride in New York City. As he was paying the driver, he said, "Thank you, sir." At this the driver leaped, ran around the back of the cab, and opened the door for his passenger. Startled, the man got out and said to the cab driver, "You didn't have to do that," to which the driver responded, "I wanted to. You are the first person in this country to honor me by calling me sir, and I thank you for that respect." The man had never before considered the power inherent in a respectful gesture, but from then on, kindness became the pillar upon which he built his life and the legacy he hoped to pass on to his children. That exchange, he said, changed his life. He understood at the deepest level that we are all the same—an invisible "fact" of power.

Here are some other invisible facts that you can review when your spirit needs a reminder of the great power you have with which to make a difference in the world.

1. FACT NUMBER ONE

Life Is a Spiritual Journey

Vest yourself in the belief that your life is a hero's journey of spiritual progress. Mapping your way along the spiritual coordinates of purpose and compassion will help you navigate the storms of change. Life will never be a logical, rational, controllable experience. Some events and relationships will enchant us and others will crack us wide open with pain. Some people might win the lottery and others may end up broke through bizarre twists of fate, but we cannot outrun or outsmart the winds of change. Know that underlying the storm is peace, and under the chaos is order. Use the power of faith as your anchor: faith that there is a reason why things happen as they do; faith that you will make it through a crisis; faith that you are moving forward to a better place.

Whether you are the one in the orbit of change or whether you are helping another person through a cycle of endings and new beginnings, recognizing a crisis—no matter what that crisis may be—as the spiritual experience of "endings and new beginnings" opens up a profound channel of light and grace. One of the most empowering acts of service is to believe in someone when he lacks the faith to believe in himself.

The following story tells how naturally people can channel grace to someone in despair. Writes Donna B.: "Years ago I hit a rough patch and was facing the Christmas holidays broke, underemployed, and alone with my one-year-old daughter—or so I thought. My family was far away and unsupportive of my recent divorce and therefore not inclined to help me arrange a trip home for a holiday celebration. I was a bit too proud to tell friends how serious my financial situation was so I kept it to myself—chin up and working as hard as I could to keep money coming in fast enough to keep a roof over our heads.

"One night, five days before Christmas, there was a loud knock at the door late in the evening. When I answered, no one was there, but on the front porch was a gift-wrapped package with my daughter's name on the card. The next day when I arrived home from work, I noticed that the front door dead bolt was unlocked. I was a bit hesitant to enter. I peeked inside and saw a large box on the couch surrounded by several bags with Christmas tree lights spilling out of them. Someone had "broken" into my home during the day and left an artificial tree and all the trimmings for me. That night there was another knock and I ran to the door hoping to catch my Santa Claus, but I wasn't fast enough. More gifts for my daughter and me were on the steps. This continued right up until late Christmas Eve. My precious baby and I had a beautiful holiday complete with music, a tree and all the trimmings, holiday food, and toys and gifts for her. I was stunned and deeply touched. I started asking around about who might have done such a touching thing, but everyone kept quiet. It took weeks for the whole story to unfold, but six people contributed to my holiday joy and through their generosity, helped me to break through the despair that had gripped me. None of them, incidentally, know about the others. They had all acted independently. I will never forget how this experience made me feel. I am certain that we are never alone and only need to recall this time to remember it again."

2. FACT NUMBER TWO

Your Biology and Your Spirit Want to Serve

It's impossible for your body to live separate and apart from the journey of your spirit. Giving makes you feel good; not giving makes you feel bad. Developing compassion and an open heart is good for you and others. His Holiness the Dalai Lama says that as a child, he was as angry as any child and even a bully at times. But after sixty years of meditating and developing compassion, the angry emotions faded away. He doesn't even have to work to suppress any anger; he simply never even feels it.

Following your intuition is vital to your own empowerment and to your physical and spiritual health. All paths of enlightenment direct us to search within ourselves for the right energy to channel to others. Our highest potential cannot be tapped without a commitment to reaching out to others. Service is the most powerful act.

A Personal Act of Power

Increase your attention to your body, especially when you are in need of help or around someone who is reaching out to you. Learn to interpret your physical sensations: they are generated by your intuition. These sensations will direct you to decide whether you should help, how much you should help, and when to say no. At the very least, however, respond with a prayer.

Your biology can also signal you to help in ways that are completely foreign to your normal responses. Often your body registers the heightened vibration of healing grace long before your mind and emotions are conscious that you can channel healing energies.

I love this letter because it is a perfect example of how a man paid attention to the signals in his biology and responded to a person in distress in a completely unfamiliar way. Writes Sally: "Thirteen years ago on our way to research elephants in Zimbabwe, my husband and I visited Egypt. During a cruise on the Nile we met a fellow Australian couple just retired after a lifetime of hard work. Also on board was a group of orthopedic surgeons from the USA. They drew to our attention that the wife had scraped her ankle and contracted an infection that they feared was close to poisoning her blood. They were recommending that this couple leave the boat so she could be admitted into the hospital. Now this incident developed only ten days into their longed-for trip, which was to last another three months. This shy couple was desperately upset and frightened at the thought of going to a foreign hospital. But there seemed no other option, as antibiotics were not working and red streaks had begun to manifest on her leg. Eventually she was unable to put her grossly swollen and discolored foot to the ground.

"I watched as my usually reserved husband started to speak with this woman, and then he stretched his hands over the wound for some time. He had never done anything like this before or even discussed such things. His father had been a well-known doctor, but my husband had shown no inclination to follow in his footsteps; quite to the contrary, in fact. To say that I was startled by this is an understatement. To my shame, I have to admit that if anything, I was mildly embarrassed. Afterward I asked him what he had done. He said he had no idea why but he felt an undeniable urge to say to the woman that he felt he could help her. And then he felt directed to hold his hands in place over her wound. He said that a thought came into his mind that he should ask for healing to come through him to her. He said it had nothing to do with him, that he was simply a tool. He said that heat began to pour out of his hands and that he knew when to stop the process because his hands cooled down. Well, this large, macho, Aussie male smiled after what he had done and we let it go. The doctors, I have to say, were doing a lot of snickering.

"The couple did not come to dinner that evening. At 5 a.m. the next morning there was a knock on our cabin door. There stood the couple beaming smiles that lit up the room. The woman was ecstatic. She said that immediately following the hands-on episode, she had felt great pain, so they decided that the next day they would return to Australia for medical care. This would be the end of their dream trip. They were desperately sad and frightened as they sat in their cabin that previous evening. When she woke in the morning, the red streaks had disappeared and a crust was forming over the ulceration. The heat had gone from the wound and her temperature was now normal. Well, you can imagine that I was amazed, although oddly enough my husband accepted the news as if it were commonplace for him. The group of surgeons was equally startled but still encouraged the couple to leave the cruise. They didn't. In fact, they were able to enjoy the rest of their trip.

"It was bliss for us to be a part of that event and it was also the start of a new and extraordinary way of life for my husband and me. It hasn't been easy, as that marked the beginning of a shift in our attitudes, beliefs, and lifestyle."

3. FACT NUMBER THREE

Intuition Influences Every Choice You Make in Life

You are an intuitive being. Intuitive abilities are as natural as breathing; they are not enhanced by diet, incense, or aromatherapy. Your intuition evolves along with your sense of self-esteem, which develops as a by-product of learning how to survive. Your spiritual life enhances your self-esteem and gives you a sense of purpose, which in turn builds your confidence in your ability to survive. That feeling that you can "handle" life—a sensation not based upon the accumulation of wealth or power, but on your spiritual instincts—gives you the mental, emotional, and psychic resources essential for strong intuition.

The goal of your individual hero's journey is to allow your intuition and spirit to become your dominant sources of power. I chose the following story because in addition to the profound spiritual support this woman provides to the elderly in her care, her description of herself reveals that she has a healthy sense of her intuitive parameters. Writes Jennifer B.: "As a nurse/social worker, I often sit with people in their living rooms or at their hospital bedside in the middle of a crisis. Many times I talk from another place inside that I know is my higher self. I never know what may come out, but I serve people in this way. They listen to the information and many times feel better as a result. I am not counseling them. This is different. Sometimes I am the only person that speaks about their impending death or their loneliness.

"One ninety-eight-year-old asked me, 'Jennifer, how do you die?' I said, 'Well, Linda, I don't remember, but I think with you, it will be gentle and quiet. You have to remember to try and not be afraid.' She liked that and we talked about wonderful things, simple things. Here's the kicker—I leave feeling like I have been with remarkable beings and I am so humble to be with them. I am honored to assist them. As I serve, I learn how to grow old, how to die, how to love my life and understand more deeply how sacred life is. I serve as a messenger, but I serve people who are great and honored beings who are loved and cherished by the divine. If the endearment that I feel is a fraction of what the angelic consciousness feels toward all sentient beings, than that purest of feelings must be overwhelming. I don't know how long I will be of service in this manner, but I love every assignment I get. Mind you, some of these people are cussing and delusional. I've been hit and spat upon at times. But somehow the luminous beauty of their souls shines through."

A Personal Act of Power

Know your intuitive boundaries. Pay attention to both your biological and your intuitive signals. Remember that just because you can sense that someone is in need does not mean that you are the one meant to help him or her. You must ask yourself if you are psychically prepared for the type of assistance required and if not, assist with a prayer and a loving thought. I learned as a matter of my own emotional survival years ago that I cannot possibly do the number of intuitive medical readings that I am asked to do. For the longest time, the guilt was so great that I could no longer even read the letters that poured into my office from all over the world. Finally I began to pray for each one, asking that the divine send someone to them who could help them because I could not. Prayer is powerful medicine.

4. FACT NUMBER FOUR

Your Intuition and Generosity Evolve as Your Personal Power Evolves

Generosity is an expression of our spiritual maturity. I will remind you of the very revealing comment one gentleman made to me, "I would give my friend money to help him get by in life, but not to pass me by." What we have to learn, which this man has not yet, is that empowering someone else empowers all of humanity and ourselves at the same time. When we truly understand that, then we will not hesitate to help someone else.

We go through four stages of learning generosity: tribal (first and second chakras), personal (third), intimate (fourth and fifth), and spiritual (sixth and seventh). This scale of ascension is very, very real. What you are capable of doing for others is as important to understand as what you cannot bring yourself to do. To empower someone's spirit requires that you have empowered yourself, confronted your fears, and realized that your personal power will not be diminished. Otherwise, you are working from the "shadow side" of generosity.

For instance, I had a conversation with a man whose son was constantly trying to "win"—his choice of wording—his approval. I asked him why his son had to win his approval—what would it take? He smirked and replied, "He has to win my approval because that keeps him in his place. But he will never win my approval until I am old and gray, because I never want him to ignore me." The son continued to run a race he had already lost, because his father is too insecure about his own survival to empower his son.

The following story illustrates a deep understanding of what true empowerment entails. Writes Naomi D.: "My son, age seventeen at the time, had already attempted suicide twice. He had been hospitalized and was in the care of both a psychologist and a psychiatrist. The pattern was that he would pick an argument with me and that would be his excuse to act out. One Saturday evening when my husband was at work and my daughter was asleep, he started pushing my buttons. As I became aware of what was happening, I decided that I would not become involved in the drama and that I would leave him to do whatever he decided to do. I would not stop him again. I knew he was going to attempt suicide. It was one of the hardest things I have ever done but in making my choice I was placed and held in an amazing state of grace. My son left home and did attempt suicide that night, but found help by contacting the doctors who were counseling him. It was his last attempt. He is now okay. He performed an amazing act of service for me by bringing me to the place where I had to surrender—to let go and let God. Before he left the house, I came to peace within myself knowing that no matter what the outcome was to be of that evening, it would be according to the divine plan and not mine. I accepted that. I have found this to be the greatest act of service performed for me because now, when I find myself losing faith, I remember that feeling of being held in grace and it always touches me. On discussing that evening with my son several months later, he told me that I had given him the most wonderful gift that evening. He got to choose for himself whether he should live or die. He found that he could take care of himself—survive—without looking to his mother or father to fix things for him. This gave him feelings of self-worth and self-esteem and although at the time he did not know how he would be able to manage his life, he knew that he wanted to live."

A Personal Act of Power

All forms of service essentially empower a soul. Remind yourself that you can provide this power in many ways: encouragement, hope, kindness, and a nod of approval.

5. FACT NUMBER FIVE
Angels and Grace Are Real

And that's just a fact of life. Period.

I love this story of a vulnerable woman who still acted as an "angel in disguise." C. C. writes: "I was in Russia for a conference, having arrived late at night at the Moscow airport. Foolishly, I did not have any cash on me, only traveler's checks, which are useless in a closed-down airport. I had no idea where the people were who I was supposed to meet and had no way of finding out. I ended up hopping into a car with a man posing as a cab driver who wanted to be paid in goods that I could purchase from the hotel kiosk. I managed to communicate to him the hotel I needed to go to. I was so frightened that I would have promised him two weeks in Hawaii with his wife if I thought it would get me to a safe place. When we finally made it to the hotel, I was informed that they did not have a reservation for me or any spare rooms. The woman at the hotel offered me a hard, metal chair for the night.

"Not knowing what to do, I wandered into the lobby and just stood there, frozen. Then I heard a man speaking English. I approached him and explained my plight. He excused himself for a moment to speak with two women and then returned, telling me that those two Canadian women were fine with me sleeping on the floor of their very tiny hotel room for the night. I was never so grateful. I went to their room and between their luggage and mine, the room on the floor meant to be my bed for the night was four feet long and two feet wide. Still, it looked like a suite at the Ritz by this time. These two women asked their interpreter to go down to the woman in charge of the floor and ask for an extra blanket and pillow. Shortly, this interpreter returned announcing that a Russian woman staying in the hotel had overheard the interpreter's request for a blanket and offered the spare bed in her room 'to the American.' Next thing I know, I was in the room of another stranger, still scared and, by this time, hungry. This gentle woman noted my stress. She rummaged through her luggage and pulled out a box of chocolates. I immediately knew it was a gift—and that she had probably had to wait in line for six hours to buy it—for her family, but she was generous enough to open it for me. As she moved, I noticed that she was protecting her right side. I pointed to that area, and she communicated to me that she had just had surgery for a tumor. It's amazing how well two people can communicate who don't speak the same language. When she had opened her luggage, I noticed her wardrobe and it was apparent to me that she had few items of clothing. I wanted to thank this woman, who had become an angel to me, so I opened my luggage and gave her every spare piece of clothing I had. Her eyes filled with tears, as did mine. In the morning, we parted, but

I will always remember her with such love. Few days have gone by in my life that I do not recall the face of my Russian angel with love, gratitude, and a prayer."

A Personal Act of Power

Believe in the presence of angels and in the power of grace. Notice and appreciate synchronicity. Keep an open mind that divine forces are at work in everything that happens to you, whether delightful or difficult.

6. FACT NUMBER SIX
You Are Never Alone

Of the many heartwarming comments that filled these wonderful letters, the stories in which people realized that they are not alone in this life struck me as being particularly special. This is obviously a central lesson for us to learn on Earth School. In reading all these stories, it occurred to me that the divine sends us into that place of aloneness just so that our lives can fill up again and make us realize how precious the people are who share this lifetime with us.

Equally significant is how many people noted that to have one good friend, one genuine experience of love, is enough to make life worthwhile. That is why I chose the following letter to share: Writes Patricia M.: "I was very devoted to my aunt who lived with us from the time I was born. My parents were dead and she continued to live with me and provide companionship. I had great difficulties with my brother and his wife. After my aunt died, we made no attempt to grow closer. Due to a family incident, I did not want to see them again. The holidays were approaching and I knew I wouldn't be invited to their home so I went away for Thanksgiving and Christmas. The next year I went to work as a special education supervisor. I met a lady, Tommi, who eventually became my secretary and lifelong friend. I really didn't know her well at this time, but as Christmas approached, she could tell something was wrong. She insisted I come to her house and share Christmas with her husband and four sons. I declined. I was sitting alone on Christmas Eve when the doorbell range. Tommi lives in Brooklyn and I live in Queens and there she was, insisting that I come to her house. It took quite a bit of convincing, but I finally agreed.

"It was wonderful. Presents were everywhere and everyone was so glad to welcome me. I never felt like that before. When I bought a condo in Vermont, she and her husband and sons, now all grown men, shared the skiing and summer fun. At last I had a family. We have shared everything together since that Christmas. I have just lately come to realize how God intervened to place me in that situation. I have been a part of their marriages, deaths, and births—the true cycle of life—because she extended herself in an extraordinary way to a stranger. Maybe she will never know how she changed my life. She taught me that love asks no return and when you extend yourself to anyone, Jesus is there beside you. I could never have learned that lesson without her. I have tried to make the rest of my life a model of that spirit of selfless giving without question or judgment. Now that my brother is alone, I will be there for him. I can do that because one person taught me that love is kind."

In Jesus' own words:

What does it profit, my brethren, if a man says he has faith but has not works? Can his faith save him? If a brother or sister is ill-clad and in lack of daily food, and one of you says to him, "Go in peace, be warmed and filled" without giving the things needed for the body, what does it profit? So faith by itself, without works, is dead.

But someone will say, "You have faith and I have works." Show me your faith apart from your works, and I by my works will show you my faith. You believe that God is one; you do well. Even the demons believe—and shudder. Do you want to be shown, you shallow man, that faith apart from works is barren? Was not Abraham our father justified by works, when he offered his son Isaac upon the altar? You see that faith was active along with his works, and faith was completed by works, and the scripture was fulfilled which says, "Abraham believed God and it was reckoned to him as righteousness"; and he was called the friend of God. You see that a man is justified by works and not by faith alone. . . . For as the body apart from the spirit is dead, so faith apart from works is dead.

—JAMES 2:14–26.

A Personal Act of Power

Whenever you feel that you are alone, release a prayer. Ask for help and let it go. Never underestimate how important you are to someone else. When you feel alone, keep in mind that the aloneness is a temporary place between orbits. You are in motion to another place where there will be love and new friends to meet you. That is a fact of life—and I didn't write the rules. I just know them.

7. FACT NUMBER SEVEN
Everything You Do Matters

I learned so much from all the wonderful people who contributed to this book. Their stories made me realize—truly realize at the deepest level—that everything we do, say, think, and feel matters. The world has become a different place for me.

Personal Acts of Power

There is more power in the invisible realm than we can ever imagine. The power of love, kind words, kind thoughts, and a compassionate response, are just a few of the different names we have for the energy of grace. Whenever you are in a bind or frightened, release the prayer, "Fill this moment with grace so that I can find my way," and trust in the presence of grace from that moment onward.

I've gathered a list of the invisible acts of power that meant the most to people and I share them as a to-do list, should an opportunity arise.

1. Hold a door open.
2. Smile.
3. Offer a kind word and encouragement.
4. Give a compliment.
5. Listen without interruption.
6. Make a call when your intuition tells you to.
7. Offer a prayer for a homeless person.
8. Pray—period.
9. Forgive others and yourself.
10. Prepare a meal for a friend.
11. Refrain from judging another person harshly.
12. Remember that life is full of miracles and have faith that every difficult situation can change in the blink of an eye.
13. Remember the truth that there is no such thing as a small or insignificant act of service.

14. Keep your power and attention in present time.
15. Begin and end the day in appreciation of either doing or accepting an invisible act of power.

I chose the following story to close this book because it represents the sum of the parts of this book. Writes Captain Ed: "Some years ago I attended a New Year's party in New York. I left with a goodie bag of food and as I walked to the train, a homeless young woman asked me for money. Instead I gave her the food, which she gladly accepted. I was somewhat surprised, having been frequently turned down when offering food instead of money. Even more surprising: another homeless man near me actually said. 'You did the right thing.' "

Index

CAROLINE M. MYSS is the author of the bestselling *Anatomy of the Spirit, Why People Don't Heal and How They Can,* and *Sacred Contracts* and is a pioneer and international lecturer in the fields of energy medicine and human consciousness. Since 1982, she has worked as a medical intuitive: one who "sees" illness in a patient's body by intuitive means. She specializes in helping people understand the emotional, psychological, and physical reasons why their bodies develop illness. She has also worked with Dr. Norman Shealy, M.D., Ph.D., founder of the American Holistic Medical Association, in teaching intuitive diagnosis. Together they wrote *The Creation of Health: Merging Traditional Medicine with Intuitive Diagnosis.* In 2003, she founded the CMED Institute, an educational program that specializes in intensive classes on archetypes and Sacred Contracts. She lectures internationally and around the United States regularly. She lives in Oak Park, Illinois.